LEWIS
& HARRIS

Francis Thompson

D&C
David and Charles

A DAVID & CHARLES BOOK
Copyright © David & Charles
Limited 1999

David & Charles is an
F+W Publications Inc. company
4700 East Galbraith Road
Cincinnati, OH 45236

First published in the UK in 1999
Reprinted 2001, 2003, 2004, 2005, 2007

Text copyright © Francis Thompson 1999
Photography copyright © Derek
Croucher 1999
Layout copyright © David & Charles 1999

Francis Thompson has asserted his right
to be identified as author of this work in
accordance with the Copyright, Designs and
Patents Act, 1988.

A catalogue record for this book is available
from the British Library.

ISBN-13: 978-0-7153-2721-0 paperback
ISBN-10: 0-7153-2721-6 paperback

Printed in China by WKT
Company Limited
for David & Charles
Brunel House   Newton Abbot   Devon

Visit our website at
www.davidandcharles.co.uk

David & Charles books are available from
all good bookshops; alternatively you can
contact our Orderline on 0870 9908222 or
write to us at FREEPOST EX2 110, D&C
Direct, Newton Abbot, TQ12 4ZZ (no
stamp required UK only); US customers call
800-289-0963 and Canadian customers call
800-840-5220.

Front cover image: Copyright © David
Robertson/2001 StillDigital.
All rights reserved.

CONTENTS

Half-title page: St Clement's Church, Rodel, Harris. This is thought to be a carving of St Clement himself. It is seen on the ornately carved tomb of Alexander MacLeod of Harris

Title page: Dawn over the folded red rocks at the Butt of Lewis where the visitor can see the visible evidence of the turbulence which created Lewis in far off geological times. The picture on pp 104-5 shows it literally in a different light

Left: The ornately carved tomb of Alexander MacLeod of Harris, in St Clement's Church, built in 1547. The recumbent figure is thought to be that of MacLeod himself, with lions at the foot and at the head

INTRODUCING LEWIS & HARRIS

LEWIS AND HARRIS form part of the long chain of islands known variously as the Western Isles and the Outer Hebrides, which lie off the north-west coast of Scotland. Postal addresses 'Isle of Lewis' and 'Isle of Harris' tend to give the impression that they are separate islands. In fact they are joined together by a boundary, a legal creation of a judicial decision in 1853 which no longer features on Ordnance Survey maps. The few hundred metres between East Loch Tarbert and West Loch Tarbert suggest that South Harris could in future become an island in its own right if sea levels rise as predicted in the future.

Historically, however, Lewis and Harris have gone their separate ways despite the existence of a common clan surname: MacLeod. Today they form part of the local government administrative unit controlled by the Western Isles Council, formed in 1975. In the context of their respective geography there are considerable differences, with Lewis being largely rolling moorland and Harris boasting high mountains and, in the interior, a moon-like landscape where the bare rock lies exposed to the futile attempts of climate and weathering to create useful soils. This may sound unexciting but in fact Lewis and Harris jointly form an area of outstanding scientific interest with a surprising range of flora and fauna which reflect loch systems, peaty acid soils and an alkaline machair created by

Above: The brilliant white sands at Scarista, Harris, which contribute to the fertility of the nearby machair lands where the acidity of the peat is compromised to give good growing soils

Left: Early morning breakfast for a couple of Lewis sheep, near Achmore

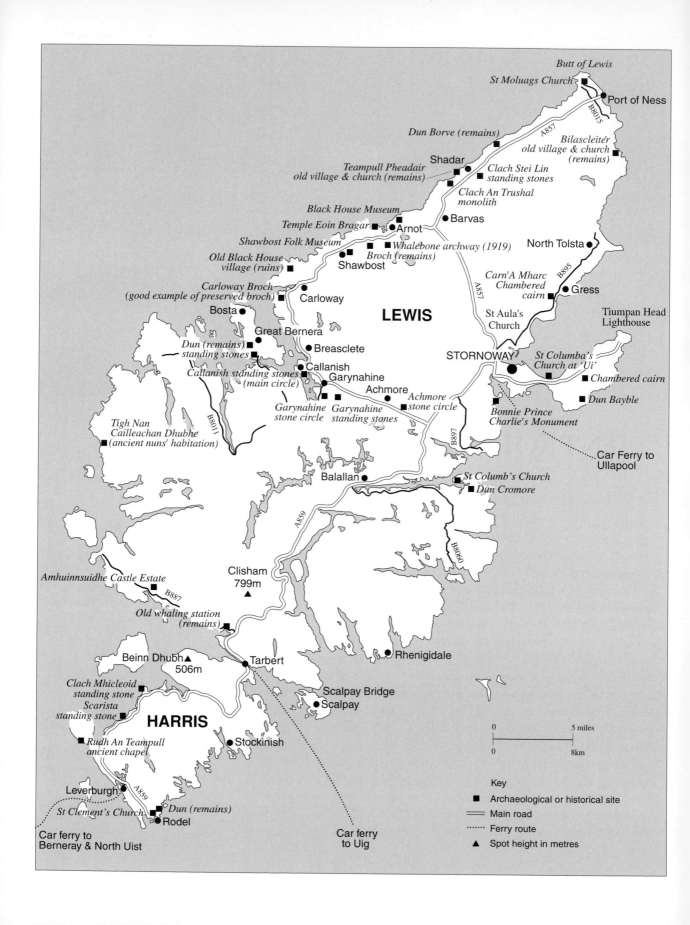

Butt of Lewis

St Moluags Church ■

● Port of Ness

B8015

A857

Dun Borve (remains) ■

Bilascleiter
old village & church
(remains) ■

Shadar ■ ●

Teampull Pheadair
old village & church (remains) ■

■ ● *Clach Stei Lin*
standing stones

Clach An Trushal
monolith

Black House Museum ■

● *Barvas*

Temple Eoin Bragar ■ ●Arnot

Shawbost Folk Museum

Whalebone archway (1919)

North Tolsta ●

Old Black House
village (ruins) ■

● ■ ■
Shawbost

Broch (remains)

Carn'A Mharc
Chambered cairn ■

B895

A857

Carloway Broch
(good example of preserved broch) ■

● Carloway

LEWIS

Bosta ● ■

St Aula's
Church

● Gress

Dun (remains) ■
standing stones ■

Great Bernera

Tiumpan Head
Lighthouse

● Breasclete

STORNOWAY ●

● *St Columba's*
Church at 'Ui' ■

Callanish standing stones ■ ●Callanish
(main circle)

● Garynahine

● Achmore

Chambered cairn ■

■ ■
Garynahine *Garynahine*
stone circle *standing stones*

Achmore
stone circle

Dun Bayble ■

Tigh Nan
Cailleachan Dhubhe ■
(ancient nuns' habitation)

B8011

B897

Bonnie Prince
Charlie's Monument

Car Ferry to
Ullapool

Balallan ● ■ *St Columb's Church*
■ *Dun Cromore*

A859

B8060

Amhuinnsuidhe Castle Estate ■

B887

Clisham
799m ▲

Old whaling station
(remains) ■

● Rhenigidale

Beinn Dhubh ▲
506m

Tarbert ●

HARRIS

Scalpay Bridge
● Scalpay

Clach Mhicleoid
standing stone ■

Scarista standing stone ■

● Stockinish

Rudh An Teampull ■
ancient chapel

Leverburgh ●

A859

St Clement's Church ■ ● *Dun (remains)* ■
Rodel ●

Car ferry to
Berneray & North Uist

Car ferry
to Uig

0 —————— 5 miles
0 —————— 8km

Key

■ Archaeological or historical site

—— Main road

········ Ferry route

▲ Spot height in metres

calcareous shell sand. It is this fertile ground, on the Atlantic side of the islands, which has provided the basis for much of the human agricultural activity known as crofting, a system of land use which is now being recognised as having potential for the conservation of the environment.

Being 'islands' they are surrounded by clean and unpolluted waters which currently represent some 40 per cent of the best fishing grounds in the British Isles. To the east is the Minch, a turbulent stretch of water which has often protected Lewis, in particular, from outside interference in an historical context. On the western side the Atlantic waters have still to be exploited to yield fish and oil. Indeed the current activity in seismic surveys and oil exploration may well provide the islands with a new and exciting sector in their economic base.

A particular feature of the landscape of Lewis and Harris is the relative lack of tree cover, setting aside the scattered attempts at tree planting of more recent dates, and the product of a determined exercise in creating woodland such as that found surrounding Lews Castle in Stornoway (c1860). But this was not always the case. The present covering of peat hides an ancient forest of roots and branches, revealed as the peat is dug up for fuel, indicating that both Lewis and Harris were once covered with native trees such as alder, birch and willow. In this way the passage of time has altered what might have been seen of the landscape by the human population over two thousand years ago.

MAPS OF LEWIS AND HARRIS

The Ordnance Survey Pathfinder series of maps (1:25000) cover all of Lewis and Harris in 21 sheets. They show highly detailed topographical information, the layout of crofting townships, main roads, secondary roads, side roads and tracks. The sites of prehistoric significance are marked and are thus very useful if one is discovering something of the islands on foot. An alternative O.S. map is the Landranger series, useful for the tourist who needs comprehensive information but in less detail.

EARLY TRAVELLERS

DESPITE THEIR RELATIVE REMOTENESS and their reputation for being inaccessible, Lewis and Harris have had many visitors through the centuries. Some, like the Vikings in the ninth century, saw opportunities for rich plunder and later community settlement. But long before the Norsemen came other travellers: those who brought goods for trading, who carried with them ideas to be adopted and adapted by the resident population, and those who promoted the Gospel message. They all left their marks on the landscape, some of which can still be seen today. In the seventeenth century the waters round the islands were described as dangerous, with rocky coastlines and no sea-lights to guide mariners to safe harbours. Yet these 'dangerous' waters hardly deterred the intrepid sailors who, in prehistoric times, were able to navigate the seas successfully. One of these voyages may well have been undertaken by a vessel carrying persons of high rank across the Minch, and was perhaps one of the craft which failed to reach her destination, because in 1991 some fishermen dredging for scallops on the sea bottom near the Shiant Isles found a splendid gold torc in their nets. Dating from around 1000BC, it is the only one of its kind associated with the Western Isles. Gold rings found at Strond, in Harris, also date from the same period and are considered to have been made from

*Guardians of their mysterious past,
these stones impress with stark beauty*

gold mined in the Wicklow mountains in Ireland. The fact that these pieces of jewellery found a final provenance in the Outer Hebrides suggests that island society then was structured sufficiently to contain aristocratic elements, and also that the waters round Lewis and Harris were frequently dotted with ships of one kind or another.

In 1982, while peats were being cut from the moorland near the Lewis crofting township of Shulishader (NB 538 352) an axe-head still set in its wooden shaft was uncovered. Radiocarbon dating places the object between 3500 and 3000BC, slotting it into the late Neolithic Age. The significance of the find lies in the fact that the axe-head is made of porcellanite, a material which is found in Northern Ireland. The provenance of the stone indicates that there was some significant sea traffic between Northern Ireland and Lewis, calling into question the notion that the seas were too perilous for regular crossings.

The existence of many early Christian sites in Lewis and Harris also indicates that the surrounding seas carried small craft navigated by the monks from St Columba's foundation of the religious houses on Iona, off Mull, intent on bringing the Christian message to the people of the islands.

It was not, however, until the years of the eighteenth century that the Western Isles attracted the kind of visitors who were beginning to appreciate that there were interesting things to discover. In particular there was the prehistoric monument of the standing stones at Callanish, Lewis, popularly supposed to be a Druidic temple. An added attraction was the fact that the islanders spoke Gaelic, offering to the traveller the chance to regale friends back home with embellished after-dinner tales. But travel was not easy and it was not until the middle years of last century that Clydeside shipping companies realised that there was a tourist market to exploit – and then within a few years the Minch was being criss-crossed by busy traffic routes to the islands.

Not all visitors went to the Hebrides for a holiday with a difference. Amateur antiquarians noticed that Lewis and Harris had a significant and visible history which could go back at least two millennia. These amateurs had an aptitude for recognising the unusual, the unique and their historical references and implications. While they charted the seas around the island, they took advantage of their spare-time freedom to survey the landscape and record the vestiges of the past which littered the scene. From these almost casual beginnings came the present-day archaeological activities which now reveal the ancient past of these islands.

TRAVELLING TO AND IN THE ISLANDS

GETTING TO LEWIS and Harris today is easy compared with a century ago. A modern roll-on, roll-off ferry (3¹/₂ hours) links Stornoway in Lewis with Ullapool on the Scottish mainland, an experience which was enhanced in 1997 by the opening of a new £8 million ferry terminal in Stornoway Harbour.

Thanks to European development money, the internal roads in Lewis are now a pleasure to use. Some roads to the more remote townships, however, are still single-track but they are easily negotiated with the frequent and strategically positioned passing places. An efficient main road links Stornoway with Tarbert, Harris, where a ro-ro ferry (2 hours) connects with Uig, Skye, across the Minch, and Lochmaddy (2 hours) on North Uist. As in Lewis, the main roads on Harris have been upgraded in recent years to make driving a pleasurable experience. A small ro-ro ferry runs regularly from Leverburgh in South Harris to Otternish on North Uist with a crossing time of one hour.

For those with an urge to fly, there are flights linking Glasgow (1 hour) and Inverness (30 minutes) to Stornoway. Internal island flights link Stornoway, Benbecula and Barra on most days of the week.

Religious beliefs are deeply held on all islands of the Western Isles, and because of this there is no scheduled public transport on Sundays. Most hotels are open to provide meals for non-residents but shops tend to be

Taking a farewell look at Ullapool as the Stornoway ferry leaves for Lewis

The ro-ro ferry Loch Bhrusda which connects Leverburgh, Harris, with Otternish on North Uist. It sails across the Sound of Harris, wending its way through a maze of islands and rocky outcrops in the Sound. Worth taking a return trip even if one is not going to North Uist

closed, as are the petrol stations. The effect of Sunday closures is to give the visitor a unique taste of a way of life which is so different from mainland Britain. It has to be experienced to be appreciated.

POPULATION

THE MAJOR POPULATION CENTRE in Lewis is around the town of Stornoway, the only major town in the Western Isles and the administrative locus of the Western Isles Council. The current population is just over 6,000, with another 12,000 living in the Lewis hinterland. The population of Harris, including Tarbert, the main centre, is some 2,200, with another 382 living on the Harris island of Scalpay. In general the people are concentrated in small townships throughout Lewis and Harris, though some of these tend to run together and give the impression of being much larger concentrations. Each crofting township is regulated by a committee which looks after the agricultural activities in the locality and, in particular, the control of the common grazing around the township.

PEOPLE AT WORK

IT OFTEN COMES AS something of a surprise to visitors that the economy of Lewis and Harris is based on a fairly broad spectrum. The common perception is that it relies on a combination of crofting, fishing and the weaving of Harris tweed. While that picture is largely correct, there are other economic activities which play a significant role in the working lives of the people. The agricultural use of the crofts, as a main or secondary activity, is still the predominant land use, though its contribution to the islands' gross product figure is declining. Less than half the crofts (average size of holding is 6 acres or 2.4 hectares) actively stock sheep or depend on Government subsidies. Much activity centres on livestock rearing and little is done in a purely agricultural context. Many crofts support a part-time income, with crofters depending on other work to maintain a reasonable standard of living.

Fishing (whitefish and shellfish), despite the decline in the fish population of the Minch waters, provides employment for more than 150 vessels in Lewis and Harris. The related industry of shellfish processing has developed over the past two decades and is now a significant area for employment. Another related industry is fish farming, mainly salmon,

Opposite: Fishing has always been an important element in the economy of Lewis. Over 30 per cent of the Western Isles fishing fleet is based in Stornoway. In recent years the income from white fishing has declined (worth £500,000), while shellfish has increased (currently worth over £3 million)

GAELIC SIGNPOSTING

When the Western Isles Council was formed in 1975, under the reorganisation of local government in Scotland, a commitment was made to give the Gaelic language a high profile in public life. One offshoot of this policy was to have road signs in both Gaelic and English initially but then to establish the use of Gaelic only. Thus, the visitor will be confronted with the names of crofting townships in their Gaelic equivalents. Those who are used to seeing the names of places on the continent in the language of a particular country will be familiar with the manner in which one can get around the islands without getting lost: using the latest Ordnance Survey maps. In Lewis and Harris the road system is not complex and it takes no great degree of intelligence to work out the places at which one stops or drives through. One map has been specially designed to give the names of places in both languages, and is readily available at the tourist offices in Stornoway and Tarbert.

Most Gaelic place-names tend to have a near equivalent English: Ceos (Keose), Carlabhagh (Carloway), Airidh a Bhruaich (Arivruaich), Breascleit (Breasclete), Tairbeart (Tarbert), Bac (Back).

At the 'border' between Harris and Lewis no customs or passports: just a hearty welcome. Harris returns the welcome on the back of the signpost

which attracts markets both in Britain and also on the Continent. The off-shore sea-cages can be seen in many of the tidal sea lochs throughout Lewis and Harris. The quality of the final of product is first-class, being derived from clean, cold and unpolluted waters. This industry, which began in the 1980s, now provides for several hundred jobs and is a major contributor to the island economy. Those employed tend to combine crofting with their secondary work.

Fish-landing activity can be seen in Stornoway, Leverburgh and Scalpay. Many boats are small and family-owned, working out of their own local harbours. Stornoway has the biggest fleet of some 50 vessels with the largest proportion being 33ft (10m) and over in length.

For many years the mainstay of the island economy was Harris Tweed. This industry had its early beginnings in Harris (hence the territorial description) and the home-produced cloth quickly became a favourite with the estate-owning classes. By the turn of this century certain production bottlenecks, such as dyeing, carding and spinning, were mechanised to cope with demand. Then Stornoway muscled in on the commercial potential, and in so doing abducted the centre of the embryo industry from Harris: today, while the cloth is still, by legal definition, woven by weavers in their own homes, the pre- and post-weaving processes such as dyeing, spinning and warping, final washing and finishing, are carried out in mills in Stornoway, Shawbost and Carloway, all in Lewis.

The highly individualistic character of Harris Tweed is legally protected by the Orb trademark and its production is ideally suited to

Tiumpan Lighthouse on the Eye Peninsula, Lewis. It was built in 1900 and is now on automatic operation. Its construction followed on recommendations that a shore watch be maintained on illegal trawling operations. In 1956 the lighthouse was fitted with a foghorn facility, with the Prince of Wales (then seven years old) being given the excitement of sounding the first blast on the new fog siren

Harris Tweed has been an economic mainstay for Lewis for many decades. By its legal definition, the cloth must be woven in crofters' homes to protect it against imitations. Restructuring of the industry has given new hope for steady employment to hundreds of weavers and mill workers. The introduction of up-to-date looms has made weaving easier and allowed for a wider range of designs than was possible on the older, traditional Hattersley looms

HI-TEC ISLANDS

In recent years advance telecommunication systems and facilities enable island people to remain within the Western Isles. There are now a number of 'tele-cottages' where people work from home. Of particular interest is the television-studio facility in Stornoway serving such TV activities as scripting, news gathering, editing and programme making. The emphasis of Gaelic in television production highlights the recognition of the language and its culture.

Information about the Western Isles is available on the World Wide Web site 'Virtual Hebrides'. Address: http.www.hebrides.com

complement other occupational activities such as crofting and fishing. Currently (1998) the industry is going through a process of rationalisation to cater for the home and international demands for this cloth. A number of weavers, scattered throughout Lewis and Harris, and particularly Harris, concentrate on production of the more traditional, heavier weights of cloth, thus satisfying the steady demand by those who prefer a significant hand-crafted element to their tweed.

Other occupational activities in Lewis and Harris include the servicing of the local Council, banks, commercial operations, construction and

THE CLIMATE

The north of Lewis lies on the same latitude as the middle of Hudson Bay in Canada. Yet the climate is somewhat milder than that of the adjacent Scottish mainland. The main influence is the North Atlantic Drift, an oceanic current which brings a large body of relatively warm water into these northerly latitudes from the Gulf Stream, and this counters the expected arctic influence. The prevailing winds are south-westerly and are mild but carry a lot of moisture. There are winters when hardly any snow is seen; if it does appear it lies for a few days only. Summers are warm, the best months being May through to August. On those days when the sun becomes really hot, a cool comfortable breeze makes outdoor excursions very pleasant indeed. In general, the low-lying nature of the landscape means that most rain-bearing clouds from the south-west blow over the islands to deposit their contents on the high mountains in Ross-shire and Sutherland on the mainland.

The Gaelic language is full of proverbs about the weather. One sums up its changing nature: Latha na Seachd Sian – gaoth is uisge, cuir is cathadh, tarnanaich is dealanaich is clachan meallainn *('The Day of Seven Storms – wind and rain, snowfall and blizzard, thunder, lightning and hailstorms').*

tourism. One particular activity dominates Stornoway harbour: the on-shore oil-related yard at Arnish which manages to fight off competition from other yards on the Scottish mainland to win valuable contracts for its large workforce. One interesting enterprise is located at Breascleit in Lewis which concentrates on research into the development of natural medicines and pharmaceutical products. In the last few years, the islands have moved away from a position of relative economic disadvantage to a situation which enables people with specialist skills to remain at home, and work through telecommuting.

1 AN ANCIENT LANDSCAPE

VIEWED FROM THE AIR when one flies to the islands from Inverness or Glasgow, the untutored eye may well see vast expanses of peaty, heather-blanketed moorland, a particular feature of Lewis, or large tracts of barren rockland as found in central Harris. On the eastern seaboard, high cliffs are firmly footed in the deep waters of the Minch, presenting a rocky platform with serrated edges which have resisted the attempts of the sea to penetrate inland. Where the sea has found weak openings, it has cut long maritime lochs into the islands' natural defences, providing shoreland crofting townships with the opportunity for fishing to supplement both diet and income.

On the western side of Lewis and Harris, particularly in Harris where the base rock platform slopes into the Atlantic, tidal waters have carved out a fretted coastline where an abundance of material, mixed organic and inorganic, has produced the means for man to settle and exploit the resource. These are called machair lands, ground which lies in shell-bearing sand and which have created fertile soil conditions. These machairs,

Above: The view from one of the satellite stone complexes associated with the main stone circle at Calanais. Peat was removed from this site in 1858. Five impressive stones form an oval with an upright stone surrounded by a small cair

Opposite: Early morning sea fog at the Butt of Lewis

19

often up to more than a kilometre wide, present a sharp contrast to the more barren and acidic soils called the 'blacklands', found inland and which are derived from glacial drift or the gneissose bedrock.

The rocks which support Lewis and Harris are amongst the oldest in the world, formed 3,000 million years ago and called Lewisian gneiss. They are metamorphic rocks which have been transformed by the heat and pressures of distant geological traumas. Gneiss appears as grey coloured but can also be dark brown or pink. It does not weather well. Some spectacular views of rock formations can be seen at the Butt of Lewis where folds in the stone leave little to the imagination as to how the rocks were formed. Only around Stornoway does a younger rock appear: a dark red sandstone which has produced good fertile soil, along with conglomerates. This local geological advantage has been subjected to agricultural exploitation over the centuries in that this land was always amenable to the horse and plough whereas in other parts of Lewis only the spade could be used to till the soil.

A typical rock-shore scene near the Butt of Lewis, with the waters of the Atlantic reasonably calm. This is Port Sto, one of a number of inlets in the vicinity

In comparatively recent geological times the landscape of the islands was subjected to the weight of a local ice-cap which wore it down to form a low-lying undulating rock platform and gouged out the U-shaped valleys of Harris and the upland parts of Lewis. The slow grinding produced broad spreads of till, thin in depth in many places but deep in others.

The Advent of Change

ABOUT 1500BC THE CLIMATE of the islands began to change. This affected not only all of the Western Isles but parts of northern Europe. Conditions became much wetter and colder and must have affected the lifestyle of the resident population of early islanders, though the rate of change was imperceptible. With the higher rainfall, which could not be lost through natural drainage and evaporation, the soil became waterlogged

Changing Coastlines

The push-pull tensions between the sea and the island coastal fringes create a dynamic picture. This is particularly true of machair areas where the work of the sea and wind continually alters the shape of the land. The most spectacular site is at Barvas, Lewis, where erosion is the most dramatic in Scotland. Another site is at Branahuie where the road from Stornoway to the Point district is always under threat, so much so that on occasions Point almost becomes an island in its own right.

At Luskentyre, Harris, the banks are constantly shifting as the result of winter storms. However, it is visitor pressure at some coastal machair areas that has led to the failure of the marram grass to maintain the integrity of the sand dunes, resulting in 'blow-outs'. An example can be seen at Borvemor, Harris, where pedestrian-induced erosion is becoming a problem between the cemetery and the beach.

Coastal shape-shifting in the Western Isles is the subject of many documentary references, going back as far as the seventeenth century, with villages disappearing, prehistoric sites being submerged and 'new' islands being created. In this respect the Western Isles share the same problems as the east coast of Yorkshire and Norfolk, where coastal erosion by North Sea incursions is a constant worry.

and its acidity level rose. This, in turn, restricted bacterial activity so much so that dead vegetation failed to rot completely and a sterile environment was the consequence.

The final product was peat which, in Lewis and Harris, formed a suffocating blanket overlying rocky hills and filling hollows and rock basins. The previous relatively fertile landscape of around 5000BC changed to present insurmountable difficulties for the early human inhabitants of the islands who could only move to the coastal littorals of the west to survive on the machair lands. This situation still exists today as evidenced by the higher number of settlements encountered along the western shores of Lewis and Harris compared with the relatively few on the eastern seaboard. On the eastern seaboard of South Harris, the townships there are a result of clearances in the last century from the machairs of the west. A tantalising glimpse of what the landscape might have looked like in times past can be seen on the small islands in lochs or in steep-sided gullies which are inaccessible to the grazing of sheep and deer.

In summary, the combination of geological events and ice-cap movements have produced a landscape which is full of interest and not without some beauty in the eye of the appreciative beholder. If one stands on a high hill one can readily acknowledge the work of nature which created vast moorland lochs stocked with brown trout, a deeply dissected landscape and, in the south-west of Lewis and in North Harris, high hills some of which dare to call themselves mountains. Some of the latter offer excellent climbing experiences with not a few challenges to those with mountaineering competence.

The Early Settlers

THE ANCIENT LANDSCAPE OF Lewis and Harris has preserved evidence of early human habitation, which is now being uncovered from the peat blanket. Some of the stone-built heritage of these first settlers in the islands can be easily seen – standing stones, monoliths and the remains of chambered cairns. These monuments go back some 5,000 years and are the visible evidence of a societal structure with an élite layer which was sufficiently influential to have these massive structures erected. Of the dwellings of the lower echelons of society little if anything remains to be seen. The people of the Iron Age period, from 200BC to c AD500, have left structures such as the duns or forts in lochs and in particular the magnificent broch at Doune, Carloway in Lewis. All these are still visible. Other early remains are now being uncovered as archaeological digs reveal what lies under the peat and under the sandy dunes of the machair coastline.

The island landscape also has its other secrets: those punctuation marks provided by historic man which are often passed without notice. Tumbled-down stones within a green-grass area on the moorland landscape mark the

old shielings to which people of the crofting townships went in the summer months with their livestock to take advantage of the sweeter spring pasture. This was once a common custom, known in technical terms as transhumance. Again, on the moorland, perhaps beside the running waters of a small stream, tumbled stones may mark the previous location of a small beehive dwelling, half underground and roofed by corbelling.

The history of Lewis and Harris, then, does not merely lie within the built heritage, the visible evidence spanning over 5,000 years. The landscape itself provides the setting, the framework within which communities adopted and adapted survival techniques and mechanisms to become established.

Perhaps the underlying moorlands of Lewis and the bare rocky expanses of Harris, the fertile machairs and the rolling hills are not so inarticulate after all, but tell a fascinating story of human endeavour and occupation which an understanding ear and eye can appreciate.

Silent sentinels at Calanais, Lewis: markers on a landscape which has seen prehistoric peoples come and go, yet the stones remain

2 THE NATURAL HABITAT

DESPITE THE UNPROMISING NATURE of the peat-covered moorlands of Lewis and Harris it does produce a habitat for many species of animals and plants. All have adapted to the island environment with significant success and even 'imported' species like mink have managed to establish themselves to such an extent that they now pose a threat to nesting birds and freshwater fish.

Peat, of course, is the dominant feature of the inland landscape, relieved only by hundreds of freshwater lochs which carry brown trout. These rarely come bigger than 12oz (350g) in weight, though the occasional 'whopper' is caught. Rainbow trout are an introduction of a number of years ago, adding variety to the angler's bag.

The peat forms a shallow skin from a fibrous type of soil derived from dead plant material. Because rainwater is not drained away efficiently, soil acidity tends to be high, restricting bacterial activity with the result that the dead vegetation does not rot completely. Peat is not an inanimate material, however. It first began to appear in the islands when climatic changes occurred around 1500BC and has been growing in bulk and extent ever since. When the Callanish Stones attracted the interest of Sir James Matheson, who purchased Lewis in 1844, he ordered the removal of peat deposits around the monument. At the beginning of the operation, in 1854, only the tops of the highest stones were visible. The smaller stones had all but disappeared. Well over three feet (a metre) of peat was removed and by 1857 the monument was exposed to something akin to its original glory, and revealing the existence of the central burial cairn.

On the drier areas of peat one comes across the ubiquitous heather, cross-leaved heather and various types of moss. In the wetter parts rushes, sedges and bogbean abound. Other species of flora include bog asphodel, deer grass and the common bog cotton or cotton grass. The insect-eating sundew is among the common peat-land flowers.

Left: The saltings at Northton, South Harris. Apart from sheep seeking their daily intake of sea-salt, these marshes are important for shore birds and wild flowers

Overleaf: The often rocky shoreline in Uig, Lewis, at times gives way to broad, sandy beaches, a popular destination for locals and visitors alike

Right: Proof that the Lewis scene is not all browns and monochromatic. This is at Loch Tiumpan on the Eye Peninsula, on the way to the Tiumpan Lighthouse

Below: A common sight on the peat-lochs in Lewis: a mallard and chicks enjoying the serenity of Loch an Tiumpan

Above: The Butt of Lewis is just the right place to see not only native birds; but visitors, migrants and vagrants, the latter often blown across the Atlantic by winds, like regular Little gulls and Ring-billed gulls

On the machairs, the rich habitat for many forms of plant and animal life is particularly diverse. This is because the calcium in the sand base has a liming effect on the peat and produces a fertile grassland which supports an astonishing variety of flowers. During the spring and summer months these meadows are almost like Persian carpets in the colours displayed by the flowers in bloom. The importance of the machairs for sustaining wildlife has been recognised by many areas being declared as Environmentally Sensitive Areas and Sites of Special Scientific Interest. Indeed, these machairs, with the juxtaposition of peaty acid soils, loch systems and their alkaline nature, makes them quite unique in the British Isles, so much so that within the whole of the Western Isles, some 40 per cent of the total land area has been identified as being of outstanding scenic value.

COASTAL WILDLIFE

THE ISLANDS HAVE BEEN deemed to be of international importance for a number and variety of breeding and migrant birds. These haunt not only the moorland but also the sea-cliffs and the offshore islands, salty estuaries and the rocky seashore. The rare and distinctive corncrake and corn bunting thrive here, having been almost driven from the British mainland by large-scale farming practices. Though woodlands are limited, except around Lews Castle in Stornoway, a few bird species manage to find habitats for breeding.

Golden eagles and merlins can be seen on occasion soaring above the moorland looking for prey on the ground. The latter includes the imported rabbit, very common on the machair lands, pygmy shrew and field mouse. There may be the occasional sighting of another imported animal, the hedgehog, particularly around the Stornoway area. The only native ground predator is the otter, a shy animal, which can at times be sighted on coastal rivers which carry a stock of salmon or trout. The existence of mink, now feral, is the result of them being allowed to escape from mink farms when the latter were closed down. This animal is a voracious predator and presents a very real threat to the breeding bird population and crofters' hen stocks. Deer occur in small herds in Pairc and Uig in Lewis, and in North Harris, with the occasional stray seen in the Lews Castle grounds.

Marine mammals are well represented, with colonies of grey seals on the offshore islands, such as Shillay off the west coast of Harris. Strangely, the colony of seals which frequent the waters of Stornoway harbour seem to survive among the traffic of fishing boats, their catches a ready source of food, as are the runs of salmon racing to the mouth of the River Creed in Lews Castle grounds to their spawning lochs upstream.

The Traigh Mhor at Tolsta, Lewis

A shady nook in the wooded policies of Lews Castle, Stornoway. Many of the trees are now showing signs of ageing and are being replaced gradually over a period of years with younger striplings which will maintain the integrity of the forest. A current programme of forestry management, under the aegis of the Stornoway Trust, will ensure the future of the woods

LEWS CASTLE WOODLANDS

IT IS IN THE variety of habitats of Lewis and Harris that the visitor interested in wild life can find much to discover. But even those who visit just to enjoy the islands, to absorb the atmosphere, to climb a hill or two, walk the moor, and stravaig over the machairs and the shoresides, will never be disappointed. Particularly rewarding is a walk through the wooded policies of Lews Castle, Stornoway, if only to pay some silent tribute to Lady Matheson who, in the 1860s, decided that the castle itself would be enhanced by being surrounded by trees and shrubs. The fact that her husband, Sir James, had connections with the Far East, through his firm Jardine, Matheson & Company (which still exists today), meant that she could obtain many species of rare trees which have managed to survive the Hebridean weather, tempered as it is with warmth from the Gulf Stream. The result today is a living monument to a determined lady.

Underlying the natural habitats of Lewis and Harris is the rock base of the islands. Generally described by the blanket term 'Lewisian gneiss', the story is much more complex with ample clues to be seen, for example, at the Butt of Lewis, and in quarries and at the rock-cuttings revealed with the recent widening of roads throughout the islands. Garnets (not of gem quality) can be found in South Harris, as can asbestos, though not in commercially viable quantities. In the mid 1990s, Britain's biggest gemstone was discovered in the Uig hills in Lewis. This was a sapphire, originally weighing 39 carats but cut and polished down to 9.6 carats. However, this was a rare discovery.

ICE AGE HERITAGE

THE PRESENT LANDSCAPE IS a legacy of glaciation, responsible for the creation of corries, glens, large island lochs and the deep basins along the coastal sea-lochs, almost akin to the Norwegian fiords. Often the movement of a succession of glaciers can be seen in the scratches or

An atmospheric view of the area near Gallows Hill in the Lews Castle grounds. This is where in medieval times the MacLeods of Lewis dispensed rough justice to wrongdoers, hence the name

striae on polished rock surfaces; they reveal the direction of flow of the ice-sheets. Often the rocky knolls seen on the moorland look like stranded whales, hence the term 'whalebacks' and *roches moutonnées*, the latter appearing like grazing sheep among the heather. These are the products of ice-flows and are common in the eastern part of South Harris. Large boulders are frequently seen on hill tops; they are the result of retreating ice having dumped them at random after the underlying soil or till was washed away. Some spectacular perched blocks can be seen at Manish in Harris.

On the coast, there is ample evidence of the work of glaciers running into the sea, the result of three glacial periods which are associated with the Western Isles. The last glaciation left some geo-

Opposite: Sea-worn stones on the beach at Shader Point, Lewis, mainly Lewisian gneiss, and showing the composition of the rocks

logical evidence at Tolsta Head (Lewis) which has been dated to about 28,000 years ago, and was a visitor from the Scottish mainland across the Minch. Lewis and Harris were both covered by a local ice-sheet about 18,000 years ago.

With the melting of the ice, the sea-level began to rise and new shorelines were created. At Galson, West Lewis, for instance, there is a raised rock platform. Other similar gravel beaches occur at Sheshader and Bayble in the Eye Peninsula of Lewis.

Whilst the subject of geology is not everyone's cup of tea, it has to be said that one cannot escape the products of the many natural forces which have formed Lewis and Harris. It is the diversity of the landscape and seascapes which add a not insignificant element of interest as one travels throughout the islands. For example, the estuarine salt-marshes at Northton and Luskentyre in Harris, and at Holm, Tong and in Uig in Lewis, formed more than 5,000 years ago, are worth looking at, if only for the bird and plant life which they sustain.

In summary, those who dismiss the Lewis landscape as dull and dismal moorland, and that of Harris as lacking in interest, might be well advised to take a second look and be well rewarded.

A waterfall near Tolsta, Lewis. Despite the often forbidding bleakness of the Lewis moorland, one comes across a scene like this which delights the eye

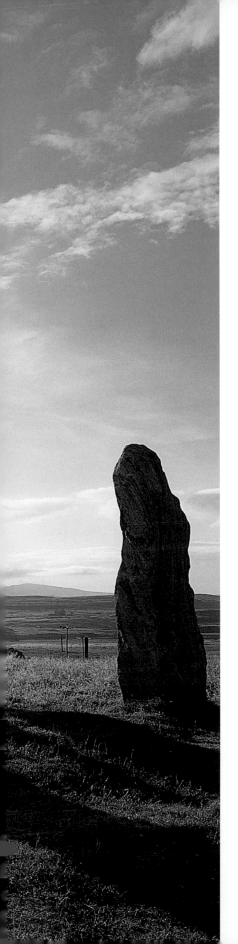

3

HUMAN FOOTPRINTS

AROUND 5000BC THE PEOPLES of the Middle Stone Age (Mesolithic) began to appear on the western coasts of Scotland. They were nomadic hunters and food gatherers and had a preference for living near the shorelands where plenty of shellfish was available. By around 3000BC these early people had become more settled in communities, raising crops and domesticating animals. Known as Neolithic or New Stone Age, they became the first farmers, ready to absorb new ideas brought by other nomadic peoples. Their relatively settled life brought an element of welcome stability and the opportunity for development of both culture and intellect. That the latter was a characteristic is seen in the fact that from c 3200BC to around 2000BC societal evolution and stratification produced a system which was sufficiently structured and organised to be able to build monuments of tall standing stones which are still visible today in the island landscape.

These New Stone Age people were more than likely the first humans to populate the then relatively attractive landscape of the Western Isles. Pursuing their agricultural practices they cleared scrub woodland and established pastures. Patches of land were cultivated. Domesticated sheep, cattle and goats provided meat, and skins for clothing. Wild deer roaming in the wooded areas gave the people an additional supply of meat, sparing the need to kill off the community's stock of animals. Shellfish from the shores augmented the diet. Fish may have been caught by trapping them in artificial pools at tidal flows, then damming them as the sea ebbed away.

Tools and weapons came from the bones and horns of hunted animals. Fine-grained stones, easily sharpened, were made into axe-heads fitted to wooden handles. Flint, so common as an edging material in the southern part of Britain, was rare in the islands, though pebbles of flint might sometimes be found on the shore. Otherwise quartz was used, as was baked shale, a rock imported from Skye, as evidenced by relics found at Callanish, Dalmore and a few other sites in Lewis. The axe-head made from porcellanite, a stone material which is found in Northern Ireland and uncovered

The Standing Stones at Calanais, Lewis: carbon-dating indicates that they are older than Stonehenge

TREES

At first sight Lewis and Harris seem to be bereft of trees, but this is not quite the case. In the eighteenth century many landowners planted trees near their houses to get some shelter and to relieve the barren landscape. The most successful attempt was the woodlands of Lews Castle, Stornoway. There are twenty-eight conifer species, thirty-nine broad-leaved species, of which fifteen are native, and twenty-four shrub species of which nine are found in woodlands on the Scottish mainland. There are a number of more exotic species, such as Chilean pine.

Other policy woods can be seen at Horgabost, Borve and Rodel in Harris. Most of these have grown in severe exposure conditions and now offer habitats for birds and other wildlife.

The Forestry Commission established trial plantations at Balallan and Valtos, Lewis, between 1945 and 1948, and, later, at Achmore, Lewis. These have been ravaged recently by the Pine Beauty Moth which killed the lodgepole pines, the devastation being seen to great effect on the plantations near the road from Achmore to Garrynahine.

during peat-cutting at Sheshader, Lewis in 1982, suggests that there existed some kind of sea-borne trade in domestic tools and implements.

How these early communities were organised, socially and for communal activities associated with the rituals derived from their beliefs, is a matter for speculation. But there can be little doubt that some structured organisation existed which had developed to the stage where a need was perceived: to celebrate the community's past origins, its contemporary status and to provide a point of reference for future generations. The manifestation of this need was the construction of major monuments such as standing stones and circles and chambered cairns.

The most spectacular monument in the Western Isles is that at Callanish, Lewis, the design of which, over a long period of time, may have had input from sea-borne travellers to produce the 'family' resemblance between Callanish, Stonehenge and Avebury in England, and Carnac in Brittany. But there are other monuments which offer the present-day visitor lithographic evidence of the distant past and its human occupants. Throughout Lewis and Harris are scattered monolithic and multilithic structures still visible after so many millennia. Some have only been discovered in the 1990s and others no doubt lie under the peat blanket waiting for exposure in the future by a fortuitous accident or by careful surveying and exploration of the landscape. For instance, in 1991 a 'new' stone circle was discovered some 5 miles (8km) south of Stornoway (NB 382 305) close by the A859 trunk road to Harris.

So far, little has been discovered of the domestic dwellings of the Neolithic people, though remains at Northton, Harris, give some hope that other sites may be revealed in time.

SOME SITES TO VISIT

Clach Stei Lin – Airidhantuim, Lewis (NB 397 546)
A stone 5ft (1.5m) high, but not entirely alone. A survey carried out in 1914 identified a number of prostrate stones, some lying under the peat, giving the impression that they were overthrown standing stones and might have been part of an original circle.

Clach an Truiseil – Ballantrushal, Lewis (NB 375 538)
This is the tallest standing stone in Scotland and may well have been a prehistoric sea marker. The coastline hereabouts tends to be rocky but the beach close by is one of the few amenable landing places available for

The Clach an Truiseil near the township of Ballantrushal, Lewis. Standing nearly 20ft (6m) high it is thought to have been a sea marker in prehistoric times, though it predates a local tradition that it was erected to commemorate a bloody battle between the Morrisons of Ness and the MacAulays of Uig

A FORTIFIED COAST

Recent surveys by archaeologists on the west coast of Lewis have revealed what is thought to have been a chain of over fifty coastal forts. Accurate dating is uncertain but the age of the fortifications seems to range from between 2000BC to AD1000. Norse-type pottery has been found at some sites, while Neolithic evidence has been unearthed at others. It is not known yet whether the forts were part of an organised protective network or were built by individual communities for fortified shelter in times of trouble from speculative and opportunist invaders.

Opposite: The remains of the Neolithic chambered cairn at Steinacleit near Lower Shader on the west coast of Lewis. Dated around 3000 to 5000BC, the cairn stands within an oval precinct which is 270ft (82m) at its largest dimension

sea-going craft. Local tradition has it that it marks the grave of a Norse prince, but also that it commemorates a victory of the Morrisons of Ness over their sworn enemies the MacAulays of Uig. The monolith, however, predates any event AD.

Steinacleit – Lower Shader, Lewis (NB 396 541)
This site has the remains of a chambered cairn with upright slabs which are arranged in a circle about 50ft (15m) across. The dating for this monument is 3000 to 500BC. With Clach an Truiseil, Loch an Dun and Clach Stei Lin all in the vicinity, the site suggests some special significance for prehistoric people of the area.

Stone Circle – Shawbost, Lewis (NB 235 462)
This site, in a distressed state, is still identifiable as a multilithic monument.

Kerb Cairn – Breascleit, Lewis (NB 218 348)
This site was revealed in 1995 when the Local Authority decided to straighten out a sharp bend in the road almost opposite Breascleit School. The site has an alignment with the double-row avenue of Callanish. In the centre of the cairn was a small burial cist which contained a cremation in a broken cremation urn. The stones forming the two kerbs are being reconstructed close by.

Chambered Cairn – Garrabost, Lewis (NB 524 331)
This site is known locally as the Hill of Doors and comprises a number of large boulders surrounding a denuded chamber area. A bit of imagination is needed to reconstruct the original monument. Its location, overlooking Broad Bay, seems to be more than fortuitous. It has an interesting line-of-site relationship with other prehistoric sites on the Eye Peninsula – Clach Stein, Cnoc Chailein at Shulishader, and Caisteal Mhic Creacail.

Stone Circle – Achmore, Lewis (NB 317 293)
This site is an example of the manner in which the prehistoric past of Lewis is slowly being uncovered by the time-honoured process of peat-cutting. In the 1930s there was a local tradition that there might be a stone circle in the vicinity of the crofting township of Achmore. Fifty years later the tradition came to life with the discovery of a circle of recumbent stones. Whether the stones fell before the first growth of peat occurred or were toppled deliberately is not certain. Research suggests the circle dates between 3390 and 2050BC, which makes it older than the Callanish Standing Stones. The site is about 656ft (200m) from the road just before the Achmore junction, where the road meets the A528.

Chambered Cairn – Horgabost, Harris (NG 047 966)
This site comprises a largely central slab which may have been the roof of

the original chamber, perhaps supported by the surrounding stones of which four are still in an upright position.

Standing Stone – Horgabost, Harris (NG 040 972)

This monolith stands in glorious isolation on a grassy hill overlooking the Sound of Taransay. It is called Clach Mhic Leoid (MacLeod's Stone) and is about 10ft (3m) high supported by packing stones at its base. One obvious function of the stone is as a prehistoric sea marker but there is a quite acceptable theory that the stone was part of a prehistoric calendrical system. Some 40 miles (64km) to the west, the island group of St Kilda can be seen on a clear day. At the equinoxes, the sun sets exactly due west over St Kilda as seen from the Clach Mhic Leoid.

THE CALLANISH COMPLEX

A worthy rival to Stonehenge in the south of England, Callanish is quite outstanding, not only the main site but in the context of the many smaller stone circles within the Callanish area. Callanish consists of a stone circle, a central monolith and five radiating rows of stones. The two rows of stones which form an avenue, aligning almost true north, links with Stonehenge, Avebury and Broomend of Crichie in Aberdeenshire. Both

The beach or 'traigh' at Horgabost, Harris, with the island of Taransay beyond. Close by is the large monolith known as Clach Mhiclieod, MacLeod's Stone, and the remains of what might be a chambered cairn of Neolithic vintage. The cairn is known locally as Coire na Feinne, based on a tradition that it has a connection with the legendary Irish warriors whose leader was Fionn mac Cumhaill of around the third century

Opposite: One of the Calanais satellites Cnoc Ceann a' Ghearaidh. The site lies within sight of the main Calanais circle and is near the shore of the inlet close to Tob nu Leobag. It consists of an ellipse of seven stones, two of which are prostrate, with a ruined cairn near the centre

This site is known as *Cnoc Fillibhir Bheag*. There seems to be a double circle, the inner represented by four erect stones and the outer by eight standing stones, including five recumbent. The stones fit roughly into two ellipses

CALLANISH – OLDER THAN STONEHENGE

Charcoal samples taken from the excavations at Calanais in the 1980s were recently subjected to radio-carbon dating in America. The results showed that the stones at Calanais are older than those at Stonehenge and were erected sometime between 2900 and 2600BC. There is the possibility that the first human activity on the Calanais site goes back beyond 3000BC. Previous estimates on the age of the Calanais Stones were little more than educated guesses. Now science has gone some way to indicate that Calanais was erected before the main circle at Stonehenge and is contemporary with the period of settlement at Skara Brae in the Orkney Isles.

BRONZE AGE POTTERY

On the coast, just north of the crofting township of Crowlista (NB 037 339), Uig, Lewis, the dried-up remains of Loch Guinnerso contains a complex of industrial, ritual and agricultural remains, yet to be interpreted. There are indications of a pottery-maker's workshop, fish-traps, field systems, burial cairns and drains. These finds add to the little evidence so far found in Lewis of Bronze Age settlement.

Callanish and Broomend are unique Scottish examples of a commonplace feature of megalithic sites in England.

The Interpretation Centre at Callanish, opened in 1996, has an audio-visual presentation which tells the story of, not only the Callanish main site, but of the many minor sites located around the head of east Loch Roag. Of these eighteen sites, no fewer than eleven have inter-site lines with possible astronomical significance. There are some other possible megalithic sites, including one on the island of Great Bernera (NB 168 345) and another near the southern approach to Bernera Bridge (NB 168 345). All the sites in the Callanish satellite complex have been examined to establish interrelated sight-lines, between acknowledged and supposed sites, and between them and the main circle at Callanish. Out of a possible 342 sight-lines between the sites, 220 were intervisible (65 per cent), indicating that the satellites within the Callanish complex have an intimate relationship with each other. This might suggest that the local area was of religious if not political significance in prehistoric times and may well once have been the most important place in Lewis.

THE BRONZE AGE

DEFINING THE CLOSE OF the Neolithic period is difficult, the more so in the remoter areas where changes came late or were only slowly merged into existing lifestyles and social structures and patterns. Notionally the Early Bronze Age began c 2200BC and its appearance in the Western Isles, to mark the end of an old era and the beginning of the new, was not an overnight event. Nor was it a massive influx of new people with new ideas. More likely it was the appearance on the horizon of one or two migrant craftsmen practising their new ideas and looking for patronage.

It is reckoned that the Bronze Age technology appeared in the islands around 1800BC, with the newcomers importing the distinctive style of pottery they manufactured and so were known as 'Beaker People'. Experts contend that the oval house built over an earlier settlement at Toe Head, Northton, Harris (NF 568 913), contained combs made from bone which were used as convenient and innovative tools with which pottery was decorated. In addition to the pottery, new ways of burial were introduced. These were 'cists' made of stone slabs to contain the remains of an individual often accompanied by beaker pots and quartz arrowheads, perhaps indicating the emergence of a warrior class in society. A late Bronze Age find was discovered last century at Adabrock, Ness, Lewis (NB 535 627), and dated around the seventh century BC. It consisted of bronze tools, weapons and personal ornaments.

The well-preserved remains of a Bronze Age settlement have been found at Dalmore near Carloway, Lewis (NB 213 451). Included in the finds were fragments of pots heavily decorated with intricate designs. This site adds to a very short list of Bronze Age settlements in the islands, though more evidence might well be hidden under peat.

THE IRON AGE

BECAUSE THE DATES ASCRIBED to 'Ages' tend to have very wide margins, a late Neolithic structure could be attributed to an early Bronze Age period. These terms were introduced in the late nineteenth century when attempts were being made to put some rational human context to the material being uncovered in early excavations.

The span of time generally allotted to the Iron Age coincides with the period during which the Celtic peoples provided the supreme military and cultural influence in central Europe, moving into Italy, Gaul (or France), the Iberian Peninsula and then into Britain and Ireland. When the Iron Age started to have some influence in the Western Isles is debatable but, allowing it some time to filter northwards, a date around 300BC might be taken as reasonable. Its arrival coincided with the deterioration of land productivity on account of the growing layer of peat which stultified the former fertile soils. One main consequence of this process would have been the abandonment of the former settlements and the resultant reduction in the usable land available for cultivation. One can only speculate on the levels of pressure which former communities had to endure.

One hint might be that the Iron Age is reflected archaeologically in new forms of settlement, designed for defence. In the whole of the Western Isles the archaeological record is virtually empty in the Bronze Age context, yet is represented in the Iron Age by over one hundred fortified sites. In general, stone-built forts have strong defensive walls and are usually sited in locations which offer strategic viewpoints, such as the tops of low hills or on islands in lochs to which access is gained only by a guarded causeway. The period for the forts runs from around 300BC to c AD200, though their occupation for more domestic purposes continued until post-medieval times.

Two types of structure are associated with fortifications: duns and brochs, with a tendency to interchange with each other, particularly in the Western Isles where both come under the Gaelic word 'dun'. In general, duns are smaller structures whereas brochs are much larger and more intricate in their construction.

Typically, duns are small, often circular and characterised by a dry stone wall some 10ft (3m) thick. The walls consist of rubble held together with built internal and external faces. Some contain chambers and galleries within the wall thickness and have stairways leading to the wall heads. These are, in fact, what the duns and the larger brochs have in common. Accommodation within the duns is severely limited, suggesting they were built to serve one or two families at most.

Details of the double-skinned walls of the Carloway Broch, Lewis. At their remaining highest, the walls are 23½ft (7m) and are drystone built. Two tiers of internal galleries are formed by flat slabs, the latter assisting in tying the walls together. The fact that the broch has not through the centuries been robbed of its stone might suggest that it was regarded locally with some respect

Left: Dun Carloway, Lewis. This is the best-preserved broch in the Western Isles and dates from the Iron Age, though it has seen opportunist occupants over the centuries, even up until the 1870s, according to a description: '. . . there still was a respectable-looking family living in the ground flat of the broch.'

The interior shot of the Carloway Broch shows some of the detail used in its construction and some of the building principles used two thousand years ago, indicating some degree of sophistication in the understanding of large structures. Also to be admired is the tight and very neat drystone walling which is evidence of the fact that the ancient masons were masters of their craft

49

ATLANTIC ROUNDHOUSES

This term covers several types of structure associated with the Iron Age (c 300BC to AD300) which are peculiar to the isles of Orkney, Shetland and the Western Isles, and the northern and north-western coasts of mainland Scotland. The structures include duns, brochs, galleried towers, island duns and a number of structural variants. What is striking is the basic unity in architectural and building contexts of these structures and the transition that they represent, from the massive stone monuments of the Neolithic people of the islands.

In Lewis, the outstanding example is at Carloway. This broch commands the local landscape and it is fortunate that so much of the structure remains after two millennia. But there are much less imposing and robbed-out examples littering the landscape from Lewis to Barra. They are to be found in those areas which offered a tolerably habitable environment, but which required some degree of protection from real or imagined invaders.

Many of the roundhouses could only accommodate two or three family units and thus may have been the main dwellings of an upper elite. There is evidence that these buildings came into fashion c 700BC when their spread was initiated by maritime communications. By the later centuries of the Iron Age, the structures were highly sophisticated, indicating a degree of mason craftsmanship which suggests a organised society, unified by ideas and a common culture.

Over a long period of time the techniques used in building dun structures were developed. Walls, for instance, could be built higher and galleries accessed by means of stairs contained within the hollow walls. These larger structures, the brochs, stand up to 50ft (15m) high and are tapered vertically. They are the classical Iron Age monument and span a period roughly from c 400BC to c AD300.

IRON AGE SITES

Promontory Fort – Cross, Ness, Lewis (NB 495 631)
Known as Dun Mara, the remains of this structure can still be discerned and may well have formed part of a series of defensive forts running down the west side of Lewis, of which a number have now been identified. There seems to have been an outer defence in the form of a ditch, 19½ft (6m) broad, cut from the edge of the cliffs on either side of the promontory.

Promontory Fort – Shawbost, Lewis (NB 235 474)
The site is on a strip of land jutting out into the waters of Loch an Dunan,

The remains of the fortified dun in Loch Bharabhat on the island of Great Bernera, Lewis. Radio-carbon dating suggests it existed c 650BC. Excavations have proved the structure to be an excellent time capsule from the various finds uncovered

RADIOCARBON DATES

While radiocarbon dating is not a perfect system, it is useful to provide an indication of the age of the finds associated with ancient prehistoric monuments. The following are some dates of interest:

Shulishader axe shaft (Lewis): 3149BC (Early Neolithic)
Northton bone (Harris): 3055BC (Neolithic)
Northton bone (Harris): 1974BC (Bronze Age)
Sheshader ancient field wall under peat (Lewis): 1111BC (Bronze Age) Stornoway wooden bowl (Lewis): 451BC (Early Iron Age)
Cnip animal bone (Lewis): 356BC (Early Iron Age)
Cnip grave, child burial: AD879 (Norse period)
Dun Carloway shell: AD1321 (Medieval period)

near the A858 and is easily accessible. The structure has suffered much from old age, and rubble covers much of the site. Even so, some features are still discernible.

Broch – Carloway, Lewis (NB 190 412)

This is the best-preserved broch in the Western Isles and ranks alongside those at Glenelg on the Scottish mainland and Mousa Broch in the Shetland Isles. At their highest point, the remaining walls of the broch are 25½ft (7.75m). They are double-skinned with two tiers of internal galleries formed by flat slabs, the latter assisting in tying the walls together. The manner in which part of the wall has fallen allows one to appreciate the principle used in the construction of the broch. The intramural galleries are visible as is the smooth sloping profile of the outer wall at its highest level. Also to be admired is the tight and very neat drystone walling which is evidence, if such were needed, that the ancient masons were masters of their craft.

Dun Bharavat – Great Bernera, Lewis (NB 156 355)

This galleried dun is on a small islet in the loch. The site has proved to be

THE VIKING PERIOD

To judge from the predominance of Norse placenames in Lewis, the Vikings occupied many sites in the island. As yet the physical evidence of their period of occupation in the island is scant. However, excavations are providing useful information as to the types of settlements with which they were associated. It is likely that many of these farms and villages have survived to the present day, particularly the older settlements, but have been obscured by later building in what is called the pre-crofting period.

In areas such as Bhaltos (Lewis) Viking Age burials are numerous, indicating a Norse preference for the west coastal areas of the island and suggesting that the Vikings looked to sea routes to the west rather than sailing down the waters of the turbulent Minch.

One Viking Age settlement found on the eroding machair near Barvas (Lewis) is associated with a dense midden (rubbish area) containing pottery dating from cAD1000. The site yielded evidence of grains of barley and oats, animal bones (sheep and cattle), and fish remnants. These indicate that the Barvas site was a farming settlement which supplemented its food diet by off-shore fishing

an excellent time capsule from which various objects have been recovered – scoops, pieces of heather rope, animal bones and straw – all of which have yet to be correctly assessed and placed in an appropriate time context.

Other duns can be seen at Lower Bayble, Lewis (NB 516 305), Loch Luirbost, Lewis (NB 395 234) and Cromore, Lewis (NB 400 206). In Harris the dun at Rodel (NG 050 831) has a continuous circular wall and still retains a couple of stone courses. Much of the foundations of the structure are buried. The site affords excellent views of Skye, the Sound of Harris and the Uists, which could suggest that the dun was once a defensive structure or a fortified lookout post.

THE VIKINGS

THE ANNALS OF ULSTER (AD798) record that the Hebrides and the north of Ireland were frequently plundered by Viking hit-and-run raids. One can assume that the Western Isles felt the weight of fire and sword and that their inhabitants dreaded the onset of each summer season. However, as the Norsemen realised that it was as well to use the islands as a base for permanent occupation, by about AD850 they began to settle down, to turn to farming and merchant trading. No doubt, the islands offered temporary shelter for the longships going to or returning from more profitable excursions in Ireland.

The visible evidence of the Norse presence in Lewis and Harris is, however, surprisingly scarce but there are some tangible connections. Watermills, for example, have their design and working principles based on Norse types. These can be seen, in their early twentieth century garb at Shawbost, Bragar and at Traigh na Berie (Berie Sands) in Uig, Lewis. The traditional island 'black house' (such as that preserved at Arnol, Lewis) has features which prove it to be a throwback to the Norse longhouse. At Garenin, Carloway, Lewis, a south-facing valley known locally as Liamshader, reveals the remains of structures and field which date from the Norse era (which technically ended in 1266).

At Traigh na Berie, near the crofting township of Cnip, Uig, Lewis, a cluster of five graves was discovered, possibly that of a Norse family. Humpbacked brooches and other objects identified as Norse, were found in a burial site at Valtos, Uig, Lewis.

Perhaps the most outstanding find belonging to the Norse era in Lewis was the splendid collection of seventy-eight carved walrus-ivory chess pieces, uncovered in the sand dunes in 1831 near Ardroil, Uig. The pieces, dating from the twelfth century, are intricately executed and portray kings, queens, bishops, knights, warriors and pawns, including the well-known archetypal Viking, a berserker biting the top of his shield. The originals are now kept in London and Edinburgh, but copies can be seen in Museum nan Eilean in Francis Street, Stornoway.

Recent archaeological digs on the west side of Lewis indicate that the Viking presence on the island was substantial and had some significance. But all this came to an end after King Haakon IV of Norway was defeated at the Battle of Largs in 1263 by King Alexander III of Scotland. Three years later, by the Treaty of Perth (1266), all of Norway's possessions on the western seaboard of Scotland were ceded to Alexander.

While it is likely that in the thirteenth century some well-established Norsemen left Lewis to return to the land of their forebears, many would have stayed. After all, their families had been 'naturalised' to some extent and no doubt inter-married with descendants of the original island people. Even today, it is reckoned that vestigial elements of the Norse character remain in the ancestral blood and spirit of the folk of Lewis and Harris.

The restored Norse mill at Shawbost, Lewis. These mills were once common in the islands. Though described as Norse mills there is nothing Scandinavian about them. The mill is fed by the water that flows from nearby Loch Raoinavat

THE CHRISTIAN HERITAGE

EXACTLY WHEN THE Christian Gospel arrived to make its impact on the people of the Western Isles is not known. In AD563 St Columba arrived in

the island of Iona, off Mull, and established a monastic school from which he sent itinerant priests and scholars charged with carrying the message of Christ to all and sundry, high and low. By the time the Vikings began their incursions into the Western Isles c AD800, their habit of naming places after what they saw indicated that Christianity was reasonably well established, as witness the many islands called Pabbay (Priest's Isle); eight of these islands are found in the Western Isles.

There is some evidence of stone-built chapels becoming a common feature on the landscape by about AD900, still primitive in their construction except in those places which had been identified as strategic centres, such as Rodel, Harris, Eoropie in Ness, Lewis, and Aignish in Lewis (St Clement's, St Moluadh's and St Columba's respectively). The penetration of Christianity into the Norse culture was a slow process and was often a political manoeuvre to achieve some stability in the control of a particular area. Some indeterminate records indicate that in the ninth century some precious and sacred relics were removed from St Clement's, Rodel, Harris, to Rome for safekeeping but were never returned. This suggests that the religious community at Rodel was a major centre even at that early date.

When Martin Martin, a native of Skye, visited the Western Isles and wrote up his account (which was published in 1695), he listed over twenty chapels in Lewis and Harris. Today, these range from grass-covered footings to restored buildings. A small number retain their walls to a sufficient height for the visitor to appreciate not only their construction but their former role in the life of local communities. Some of the buildings on Martin's list were in active use for worship, though it has to be said that by the seventeenth century Christianity was tainted by superstitious practices, such as that carried out at Ness, where libations of beer were made in deference to Shony, a sea god, to ensure good harvests in the following year.

Throughout Lewis and Harris observed religion was not always in accordance with the strict observations required either by the Roman Church or the established Church of Scotland. One mission, sent to Lewis in 1610, found that few in the island under forty years of age had been baptised: this gave rise to the perception that the natives of Lewis were, at the end of the sixteenth century, both irreligious and immoral. By 1811 a survey carried out by the Gaelic Schools Society revealed that, for example, in the Parish of Stornoway, the population was 'very destitute both of religious and secular instruction'.

In time, however, the religious aspects of Lewis and Harris were formalised with a spectrum of faiths now represented in the islands: Church

Opposite: St Columba's Church, Aignish, Lewis. This grave slab with intertwining foliage is a memorial to Margaret MacKinnon who died in 1503. She was the mother of John, last Abbot of Iona. The church is the traditional burial place of the MacLeods of Lewis

Left: The alms box in St Moluadh's Church at Eoropie, Ness, Lewis. It is said to date from the mid-fourteenth century. The padlock is an interesting example of Flemish work

Right: The ancient stone font at St Moluadh's, at Eoropie, Ness, Lewis. The font was taken from the chapel on the Flannan Isles, to the west of Lewis

St Columba's Church, Aignish, Lewis. Although dedicated to St Columba, who arrived from Iona in AD563, the original chapel was occupied by St Catan in the late sixth century. The dating is c fourteenth century. The internal measurements are 65ft (20m) by 23ft (7m) wide, dimensions which are common to other religious structures of the same dating in the Western Isles. In the middle of the last century there was a slate roof

of Scotland, Free Church of Scotland, Associated Presbyterian, Scottish Episcopal and Roman Catholic, along with other faiths with small congregations. There is, thus, a certain continuity in the religious history of the islands which spans a notional 1,500 years and which still pervades as a deeply entrenched aspect of contemporary life in the island community.

The following list of sites includes buildings of a recent dating, but all are worth a visit.

Holy Cross Church – Galson, Lewis (NB 434 594).
St Peter's – Shader, Lewis (NB 379 549).
St Bride's – Melbost, Borve, Lewis (NB 409 574).
St John's – Bragar, Lewis (NB 288 489).
St Aula's – Gress, Lewis (NB 492 416).
St Colm's – Loch Erisort, Lewis (NB 386 211).
Scarista Church – Harris (NF 007 928).
St Maelrubha – Northton, Harris (NF 970 913).
St Thomas's – Habost, Ness, Lewis (NB 507 641).
St Peter's – Swainbost, Ness, Lewis (NB 508 638).
St Ronan's – Eoropie, Ness, Lewis (NB 525 655).
St Columba's – Aignish, Lewis (NB 484 322).
St Moluadh's – Eoropie, Ness, Lewis (NB 519 652).
St Clement's – Rodel, Harris (NG 047 831) (see Chapter 7).

Churches dating from the nineteenth century onwards and worth a visit include:

Knock, Eye Peninsula, Lewis. A 'Parliamentary' church built in 1828.
Cross, Ness, Lewis. A 'Parliamentary' church built in 1829.
Baile na Cille, Uig, Lewis. Built in 1829.
Manish, Harris. Built c 1850 and recently restored.
St Peter's, Francis Street, Stornoway. Built in 1839 to serve the Scottish Episcopal congregation in Lewis.
St Columba's, Stornoway. Built in 1794 as the Parish Church of the town.
Martin's Memorial Church, Stornoway. Built in 1878, the building stands on the site of the birthplace of Sir Alexander Mackenzie, the discoverer of the Mackenzie river in Canada.
Free Church, Kenneth Street, Stornoway, which caters for the largest Free Church congregation in Scotland.

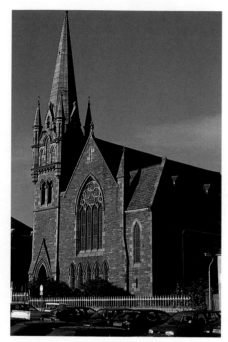

The imposing frontage of Martin's Memorial Church, Stornoway. It stands on the site where Sir Alexander Mackenzie, explorer and discoverer of the Canadian Mackenzie river, was born. Built in 1878, the spire was added in 1911 to add a note of distinction to Stornoway's skyline as seen when the ferry comes into the harbour

4 HISTORICAL TOUCHSTONES

THE HISTORY OF LEWIS pours onto the pages of the world's history in surprising ways. This chapter looks at some of the historical and cultural aspects of Lewis which might enhance the visitor's appreciation of the island which, though its situation is now changing, has until recently been reluctant to wear its history on its sleeve. (Harris is given its due place in Chapter 7.)

ISLAND CLANS

THE PASSAGE OF HISTORICAL time is not always obvious in the visible evidence presented by the stone-built heritage, from prehistoric eras to more recent years. History is also reflected in the names of islanders which have long had significant local connotations.

When Norway lost its sovereignty over the Western Isles by the Treaty of Perth in 1266 ceding the islands to Scotland, there was an inevitable jockeying for position and power on a stage already crowded with budding aspirants. In Lewis, three surnames are associated with the emergence of the island's documented history: MacLeod, MacAulay and Morrison. They owed their allegiance to the Lordship of the Isles (MacDonalds) who took possession of Lewis in 1335 and continued to keep it until the Lordship was dissolved in 1493. There was another surname present in Lewis at the time, reputed to be one of the oldest families in the island, the MacNichols or Nicolsons. All these clans were of mixed Celtic and Norse ancestry. Lesser clans included MacRitchie, Martin and MacAskill who allied themselves to whichever major clan offered some essential degree of survival and patronage.

Like many of the Highland clan surnames the origin of the major Lewis families is not entirely free from obscurity. What can be said of the MacLeods is that they claim to be derived from a progenitor named 'Leod', from the Norse name 'Ljotr'. He had two descendants, Torquil and Tormod. The former was the forebear of the MacLeods of Lewis, the Siol Thorcuil (seed of Torquil); Tormod (anglice: Norman) begat the MacLeods of Harris who are currently represented by the MacLeod of MacLeod ensconced in Dunvegan Castle on Skye. While today there are no direct descendants of the Lewis MacLeods, there are a number of claimants

Even if one's knowledge of Canada is superficial, the existence of the Mackenzie river will be well enough known. What might not be common knowledge is that the river was named after Sir Alexander Mackenzie in 1793, a Stornoway-born young man whose adventures of discovery put Canada on the world map. About twenty years later, in 1813, another son of Stornoway was in Java making an exploration of the largest river in that island, the Bengawan, from its source to its effluence. He was Colonel Colin Mackenzie who did not think to re-name the river 'Mackenzie'. Had he done so, the world might have had two Mackenzie rivers, one in the West and one in the East, both owing their names to two men, born within ten years of each other in houses in Stornoway which were only a couple of stones' throw from each other. A member of the crew of the Bounty, *skippered by the notorious Captain Bligh, was a James Morison, a native of Stornoway*

Inside St Columba's Church, Aignish, Lewis. A grave slab, now much weathered, showing a mail-clad warrior armed with a spear and commemorating Roderic MacLeod VII of Lewis, who died c 1498

NORSE OR IRISH?

A Lewis tradition suggests that the MacAulays were descended from an Irishman, Iskair, from which the Christian name Zachary is derived. While that is a matter for speculation, it just so happens that Zachary was once a common clan forename, one such being that of the Chamberlain of Lewis during the early years of the eighteenth century. Another Zachary of the Uig MacAulays was a fellow worker with William Wilberforce for the emancipation of negro slaves.

who maintain they are nearest to the main genealogical line.

There is a traditional belief that before the MacLeods took possession of Lewis, the island was in the hands of the Nicolsons (Norse: Nicolasson) who are said to have built the old Stornoway Castle (not the present-day Lews Castle in Stornoway). This fortress lasted in a ruinous state until the late years of the last century. According to another tradition, Torquil, son of Leod, gained possession of the districts around Stornoway and in the parish of Lochs, south of the town by killing off the male members of Nicolsons and 'violently' marrying their heiress. However, documented history reveals that the same Torquil received, in the fourteenth century, a grant of Assynt in Sutherland, across the Minch, and that this grant came along with his marriage to the heiress, Margaret MacNicol. But tradition has always had the more exciting stories. The MacLeods managed to keep hold of their part of Lewis until the turn of the seventeenth century when the whole island was taken over by the Mackenzies.

The area of Ness, in the north of the island, was the domain of the Morrisons, while the more mountainous area of Uig in the west of Lewis was controlled by the MacAulays. Despite their fall from grace, the MacLeods are still the most numerous clan in Lewis, turning history on its head by now being predominant in every Lewis parish, even in the districts where to be a MacLeod was certain death at one time a few centuries back.

The Clan MacAulay has been associated historically and by island tradition with Uig on the west coast of Lewis. Of Norse extraction (Norse: Olaf, Olafsson) the clan maintained control over their mountainous territory, which no doubt gave them some security from any attack by, in particular, the Morrisons of Ness. Perhaps the most famous of the MacAulays of Lewis descent was Thomas Babington MacAulay, the eminent British historian and essayist of the last century. Another MacAulay of the very same name founded the Sun Life Assurance Company of Canada. His family gave much financial support for the rebuilding of Stornoway Town Hall in 1929 after it was burnt down in 1918.

There seems to have been some 'understanding' between the MacLeods and the MacAulays, perhaps some reward for the latter not interfering too much with the formers' control of Lewis. In 1506, when old Stornoway Castle was besieged by the Earl of Huntly on behalf of the Scottish Crown, the MacAulays offered assistance to the then MacLeod chief. The offer proved to be something of a disaster for them, since Huntly's forces met up with them at Achmore, where they were heavily thrashed. Following through on their military advantage, Huntly's soldiers chased the retreating MacAulays to a place near Callanish where not even women and children were spared the sword.

During the period of the Lordship of the Isles (1336–1493) each island of any importance had its own Brieve, or Judge. That hereditary position in Lewis was held by the Morrisons with the Brieve having his quarters at Habost, Ness. The Morrisons were of Norse descent, though their Gaelic

ST COLUMBA'S, AIGNISH

The roofless four walls of this fourteenth-century church lie on a sand cliff facing Broad Bay. Though dedicated to St Columba, tradition has it that it was built on the site of an earlier hermit, St Catan, who lived in the late sixth century. Its internal dimensions are 65 × 23ft (20 ×7m), measurements which are common to other religious structures in the islands.

Documentary evidence shows it was in use as a rectory in 1506 and it continued in use for services until the 1820s. Inside the church is a grave slab, portraying a mail-clad warrior armed with spear and sword, commemorating Roderic MacLeod VII who died in c 1498. Another grave slab bears an elaborate design of intertwining foliage, a memorial to Margaret MacKinnon who died in 1503. She was the mother of John, the last abbot of Iona. These slabs are in a bad state of weathering and are in sore need of urgent attention before the carved details disappear completely.

The church and its environs were the traditional burial ground for the MacLeods of Lewis. But their arch enemy, William Mackenzie, 5th Earl of Seaforth, also lies here.

name Mac'IlleMhuire ('devotee of the Son of Mary') might suggest a different origin: on the other hand, the name may indicate that they were Norsemen who adopted a devotional style of name which was a common occurrence among Gaels.

Being a hereditary position, the Brieveship invested a significant degree of power in the incumbent and it gave the Morrisons a particular hold over the affairs of Lewis. That there existed some mutual diplomatic connection between the Morrisons and the MacLeods is seen in the relatively harmonious relationship between the two clans. Otherwise it would hardly have been to the advantage of the MacLeods to have such an authority as the Brieveship invested in another clan on the same island. The mutual trust was eventually broken towards the end of the sixteenth century when the Brieve was caught in a compromising situation with the wife of the MacLeod Chief, Ruari. The enmity which followed is recorded in Lewis traditions and saw the end of the hereditary position.

Towards the end of the sixteenth century, Stornoway saw the landing of a number of 'Gentlemen of Fife', known as the Fife Adventurers. They had been given permission by King James VI of Scotland to colonise Lewis and turn it to commercial profit. The king's report about the 'riches' of Lewis turned out to be more than illusory and the intended colonists left the island. The vacuum was filled by Mackenzie of Kintail, later called Lord Seaforth.

When the Mackenzies arrived in Lewis they had to root out the remnant of MacLeod hierarchy in the form of Neil MacLeod, a son of the MacLeod Chief. He took refuge on the small island of Berisay (now remembered in Berisay Place, Stornoway) in the Atlantic approaches of Loch Roag, on the west of Lewis. He held out for some three years before surrendering himself and his followers into the hands of MacLeod of Harris. The latter, however, probably as the result of some duress, handed Neil over to the Privy Council in Edinburgh. Neil's trial followed and he was executed at the Market Cross in that city. He died, tradition tells us, 'verie Christianlike'.

One of the first acts of Lord Mackenzie was to give tracts of Lewis land to his namesakes. He also brought in other mainland families – Mathesons, MacIvers, MacLennans and Rosses – who over a period of time intermarried with the residual population to dilute the original territorial/ surname patterns which had existed before 1610.

At the present time, however, the MacLeods still dominate the name densities in each of the island parishes, comprising some twenty per cent of the total population, a figure which has barely changed over the last century. Morrisons (originally Morison) are third on the list and the MacAulays, who were once one of the oldest clans in Lewis, cling to some 3 per cent of the island names. This decline is attributed to the widespread clearances which took place in Uig in the mid-nineteenth century; they were rarely re-occupied by their former inhabitants.

The name which is second most numerous after MacLeod and before Morrisons is MacDonald. The MacDonalds were once the family base of the Lordship of the Isles and it would be expected that the surname would feature prominently among the landowners of Lewis. But this is not the case. Even in the earliest rental records for Lewis, not one MacDonald appears. There has been much speculation why the second most numerous surname in Lewis has had such a low profile. The most acceptable explanation is that the MacDonald forebears allied themselves to the major island clans, taking the names of their protectors, but later reverted to their true surname and appearing, pheonix-like, to populate name lists. Many with another surname claim to be MacDonald, rather than say Campbell, MacAulay or MacIver. This common Highland custom of name-changing foils many attempts to discover original forebears who subjected themselves to extensive migrations to different parts of the Highlands and Islands to be subsumed under the dominant clan in the region in which they settled.

Population mobility spurred on by economic pressures in the last few decades has produced in Lewis a variegated pattern of names amounting to some 500 different surnames, not all of an indigenous origin. Even so, the domination of that pattern by the traditional names is still in evidence, perhaps indicating that the history of the islands survives to the present day in a form which reflects much older times.

GAELIC: THE LANGUAGE OF EDEN

IF THE LANDSCAPE OF Lewis and Harris can be said to be a museum, then the people of the islands are the equivalent of living depositories of an ancient history: the Gaelic language and its attendant culture. Gaelic is spoken by well over 80 per cent of the population with even higher concentrations in certain rural communities. Like so many lesser-used languages in Europe, Gaelic has had a history of continuous struggle to survive against acts of repression, suppression, and activities which are tantamount to genocide. Unlike Welsh, a sister Celtic tongue, Gaelic has not yet achieved the status of being recognised by the State as an indigenous language spoken within the British Isles.

There is no definite indication of the time when Gaelic arrived in Scotland from Ireland, but it is accepted that by the fifth century there was a considerable Gaelic-speaking settlement in the area known as Dalriada – present-day Argyll. Once the Scotti, or Irish, had entrenched themselves in Dalriada, their influence spread throughout Scotland – taking Gaelic with them – to establish new power bases. The spread of Gaelic was also aided in no small way by the arrival of St Columba in Iona in AD563. The movement through Scotland of the Columban peregrini was an important factor which increased the linguistic dominance of Gaelic, replacing the

A LANGUAGE FAMILY

Gaelic is a member of the Celtic group of languages; they, in turn, constitute a branch of the Indo-European family of languages. Thus Gaelic is a cousin to Latin, English, Russian and Urdu. The present-day Celtic languages are Scottish Gaelic, Irish Gaelic, Welsh, Breton, Manx and Cornish, though the latter died out but has since been revived.

Other Celtic languages once existed in Europe, such as Gaulish in what is now France, but are now long since extinct. These tongues spread far and wide over Europe some two thousand years ago and now exist only in place-names and loan-words.

THE PICTS

Whether the tribes in northern Scotland in around the third century AD called themselves Picts or whether their name 'Picti' was a Roman nickname meaning 'painted ones' is still a debatable question. What is not in question is that they were a powerful political force when St Columba made a journey to Inverness to meet with the Pictish king Brude. Brude held some considerable sway as far north as Orkney and no doubt had some territorial interest in the Western Isles, where control might have been administered on his behalf by a sub-king. The Picts are known today for their sculpted stones, adorned with figures, animals and geometric designs, the latter derived from the European Celtic art forms.

A couple of Pictish symbol stones found in the Western Isles suggests that they were territorial markers. On the other hand their geometric symbols, still awaiting scholarly interpretation, a crescent and a V-rod, may convey a completely different message, perhaps commemorating a significant event or a person of high status.

The fact that when St Columba visited Skye he needed an interpreter to convert an old Pict, Artbrannan, to Christianity (who died immediately afterwards!) indicates that the Pictish language was quite different to Columba's Irish Gaelic. After this, Columba's peregrini from Iona may have needed language lessons before they could convey the message of the Gospel to the people of the Western Isles.

language spoken by the mysterious Picts who held sway mostly in northern Scotland. The gradual adoption of Gaelic as a lingua franca would have stemmed from the language being associated with the successful political and ecclesiastical system which existed at the time.

By the twelfth century, the main influence in Scotland was Anglo-Norman, encouraged in no small way by Queen Margaret, wife of Malcolm Canmore, who saw to it that English took over from Gaelic as the language of the court, law and the church, though Latin was still to be the main medium of the latter sphere. Latin, in fact, has left its own legacy in Gaelic: *eaglais, ministear, sagairt, peann, sgriobh, leabhar*, are words which those with a little Latin will recognise as meaning church, minister, priest, pen, write and book.

Over centuries Gaelic as a spoken language in Scotland receded until, today, its influence as a community language is quite restricted, but it is in good health in the Western Isles. About 65,000 are professed Gaelic speakers in Scotland.

The history of Gaelic in the islands is intriguing. With the proven cultural and commercial relationship which the Western Isles had with the people of Ireland, even in prehistoric times, it is reasonable to assume that there was some common base for linguistic understanding and this may well have been a form of early Irish or Celtic. The missionaries from Iona in the sixth century and later centuries may well have found no great difficulty in their promotion of the Gospel among the islanders.

Then came the Norse occupation of the Western Isles from the eighth century, with its still recognisable legacy in the place-names of Lewis and Harris even though archaeological evidence of their physical presence is, as yet, rather thin on the ground. The occupation lasted some four centuries, a long enough period during which one might have expected Norse to have become an influential, if not dominant, element in the language of the islands, as it had in the Isles of Orkney and Shetland. Yet, despite the fact that Lewis and Harris were dependencies of Norway and were governed by a long succession of Norse kings, linguistic supremacy was not highly significant. After the Norse presence in the west of Scotland began to fade after the Battle of Largs in 1263, the original language, Irish Gaelic, assumed its former position, but not before Gaelic had absorbed many Scandinavian words. No fewer than 500 words are actually common to both Gaelic and Old Norse; they gave way to Gaelic inflection and eventually modern Gaelic names.

Thus, the linguistic landscape of Lewis and Harris is predominantly Norse, contained within a living Gaelic-speaking environment. Gaelic, however, is not merely a means of communication; it is also the immediate and accessible manifestation of a culture, aspects of which are quite unique in Europe. In its time of two thousand years it has accreted mythology, folk traditions, poetry and, of great importance, folk-tales, some of which have been accorded an international status by experts in their particular field. The corpus of Gaelic working songs (songs sung to accompany domestic and other tasks) is the largest of its kind in Europe. Much of the extant corpus of Gaelic culture has been transmitted orally from generation to generation for centuries, held in the fantastic memories of people who were illiterate in their own language, yet who could recite the great Celtic stories without hesitation, and do that without hesitation for hours on end.

As visitors to Lewis and Harris make visual contact with the built heritage of the islands, they may also be aware of the linguistic environment which has an intangible yet conscious connection with the past.

Today Gaelic is freely spoken among the islanders and is visible on public information signs, shop windows and within public buildings, even on Post Office vans. Gaelic-based festivals are held during the year, such as the Lewis and Harris Mods (musical competitions and concerts), Feis nan Coisir (choirs' festival) and special events featuring Gaelic song under the name of 'Blasad den Iar' (a taste of the West), specially designed to give visitors an insight into Gaelic music, song and story-telling.

FAMOUS NAMES

PRINCE CHARLIE

The association of the Seaforth Mackenzies with the cause of the Jacobites was to give them no little trouble with the Government. In 1719, Lord Seaforth gave assistance to the planners of the ill-fated Jacobite Rising by accommodating them in his Lewis home, Seaforth Lodge, on the site where the present Lews Castle now stands. It was, perhaps, just as well that Lord Seaforth was 'away from home' when, on 1 May 1746, Prince Charles Edward Stuart arrived at the farmhouse of Mackenzie of Kildun at Arnish across from Stornoway Harbour. He had managed to escape from the disastrous Battle of Culloden and had made his way up from Benbecula in an effort to charter a ship which would take him to France and safety.

The Government had placed a price of £30,000 on his head, a fortune in those days. The interesting, if not intriguing, aspect of this fact was that, though the Prince's whereabouts were known to the locals, no one came forward with information. While the Prince rested at Arnish, a companion went into Stornoway to negotiate the charter of a ship and, in the process, gave wind of the illustrious person staying across Stornoway bay. The town went into a state of shock and the Stornoway Volunteers were called out, thinking that a Jacobite army was about to invade the unprotected town.

It took the Prince's companion some time to make them realise that there was no army. But the people of Stornoway still refused to allow the Prince to enter the town, nor would they let any ship be given over to allow him the chance to escape. Thus the Prince had to make his way back to the Uists on foot and by small boat and, eventually, to meet up with Flora

HISTORICAL SOCIETIES

In recent years an upsurge in interest in local history has given birth to a number of historical societies (Comuinn Eachdraidh) in Lewis and Harris. Their members concentrate on gathering historical information about the communities in the area they represent. This is not as dull as it sounds. What has emerged from this enthusiastic collecting activity includes photographs, documents, recorded oral traditions, information on the past way of life and the life stories of the individuals. Much of the acquisition is on display in local museums throughout the islands where visitors are made most welcome, not only to look around but to have the displays explained, thus giving valuable insights into the remote and more recent past.

The cairn on a hill at Arnish Point just outside Stornoway. Erected in 1904 it commemorates the visit in May 1746 of Bonnie Prince Charlie to the town in an effort to charter a ship which would take him to France and safety after the Battle of Culloden. He was not successful and he returned, after a day and night, to the Uists where he eventually met up with Flora MacDonald

MacDonald who took him 'over the sea to Skye' and ultimately to freedom. History has noted that the Stornoway folk were to be credited for not betraying the presence of the Prince, even though the waters of the Minch were dotted with Government ships looking for him.

The incident is commemorated by a large cairn, easily visible from Stornoway, erected in 1904 on a hill above the oil fabrication yard at Arnish.

SIR ALEXANDER MACKENZIE

This famous explorer was born in 1764 in a house which was on the site where Martin's Memorial Church now stands, at the corner of Francis Street and Kenneth Street. A plaque on the church wall reminds locals and visitors alike of the fact. Mackenzie left Stornoway with his family in 1744 for New York, to find themselves involved in the imminent American War of Independence. At the age of fifteen years, Mackenzie entered the fur trade and the North West Company and soon made a name for himself with his talent for business. His employers were so impressed with him that he was offered a partnership on condition that he move out of Montreal and open up Canada's north-west, much of which was still uncharted.

Fired with the expectation of opening up new territories for the fur trade, Mackenzie decided to find out whether one of the two great rivers, the Peace river and what is now the Mackenzie river, emptied their waters into the Pacific. The journey through forests and the rushing waters of the eastern lands of Canada was an adventure which was to win Mackenzie the admiration of the world. His book, translated into French, was found in Napoleon's library after the latter's death on St Helena.

In 1808 Mackenzie left Canada to live on his estate in the Black Isle, near Inverness. He died in 1820 after a short illness. His achievement in being the first white man to cross Canada is commemorated in a plaque on the Mackenzie Memorial Monument at Dean Chapel, British Columbia.

COLONEL COLIN MACKENZIE

If Alexander Mackenzie's fate was to go west to win fame and fortune, the star of Colin Mackenzie lay in the Far East. He was born in Stornoway in 1754. Whether the two young lads knew each other is not known, bearing in mind that Alexander Mackenzie left Stornoway at the age of ten years, but their two families would no doubt have been in contact with each other. Colin Mackenzie's father, Murdoch, was the first postmaster in Lewis, appointed in 1752, though it was 1756 before the Post Office established its first official office in Stornoway.

Colin Mackenzie received a good education. He was to write: 'I must, however, attribute some part of the early seeds of passion for discovery and acquisition of knowledge to ideas first implanted in my native isle'. Unlike Alexander, Colin always maintained a connection with his home town. He seems to have had an aptitude for mathematics which got him work in the Customs House established in Stornoway in 1765. While in his early twenties, he was engaged by Lord Napier to do work on his ancestor's papers. The latter was John Napier who invented the mathematical tool known as logarithms. This exposed Colin to the knowledge of the Hindus relating to mathematics and the nature and use of the system of logarithms. By 1763 Mackenzie found himself appointed to the Engineers on the Madras establishment in India, involved with surveying the country. But he did more than that. He became deeply interested in Indian customs and Oriental studies.

The quality of his work in India earned him promotion eventually to the rank of Lt Colonel. His surveying of the Deccan region and Mysore produced the first-ever accurate maps of these regions. His lifetime was also spent collecting manuscripts and Indian antiquities, which still survive today in Madras and represent a unique collection. He eventually became Surveyor-General of all India before he died in 1821, leaving a fortune to his sister Mary in Stornoway, some of which she was instructed, under the terms of his will, to distribute to the needy persons in the town. Mary Mackenzie lived in Carn House, located on South Beach Street, but

ISLANDERS ABROAD

After a number of years when harvests were poor, the first of the emigrations to North America began. These continued at regular intervals, mostly on a voluntary basis, until the years of the potato famine in the 1840s, when landlords introduced enforced evictions to clear people from their estates. Many of the emigrants took their language and culture across the Atlantic and mixed with Gaelic-speaking people who were originally from other parts of the Scottish Highlands.

Both Nova Scotia and Cape Breton Island still have residual elements of the Gaelic heritage today, with music being the most dominant expression of the past. There are pockets of Gaelic speakers all over Canada who maintain strong familial links with the lands of their forebears.

The story is told of how a Chief of Police in Toronto became frustrated with his force's messages being picked up by the city's criminal fraternity. As many of his policemen were Gaelic speakers, he arranged for important broadcasts to be made in Gaelic, to the confusion of those who were tuning in for 'tip-offs'. The tactic proved to be successful and suggested that few, if any, criminals were Gaelic speaking!

demolished in the 1950s. The site is now an open garden space. A plaque on the south wall of the Town Hall commemorates Colin Mackenzie's connection with the town.

SIR JAMES MATHESON

Born in Sutherland on the Scottish mainland, James Matheson was destined to make his fortune in the Far East. The Company which he and his associate William Jardine set up, Jardine Matheson and Co, still exists today. Part of the Company's success was based on the importation of opium into China. By 1833 it was estimated that some six million Chinese, in all strata of the country's society, were shuffling around the plains and cities like ghostly phantoms. Needless to say, vast fortunes were made by both men and some of Matheson's share was used to buy Lewis in 1844. It is a matter for speculation who might have purchased the island from the last of the Mackenzies and what the history of Lewis might have turned out to be, had Matheson not purchased Lewis.

One of Matheson's first actions was to raze to the ground Seaforth Lodge, just outside Stornoway, and erect a mock-Tudor castle on the site. Today, Lews Castle dominates most aspects of the town and one cannot imagine Stornoway without its noble pile. Matheson spent a great deal of money improving roads in Lewis, from the original forty-five miles of tracks in 1844 to over 200 miles of reasonable coach-bearing roads by the time he died in 1878. He established gas and waterwork companies, along with new harbour facilities in Stornoway with the townsfolk enjoying the benefit of these undertakings. He even poured money into a chemical works which extracted tar from peat, and set up a brickworks at Garrabost. A profitable patent yard slip in Stornoway built ships and offered repair facilities to the shipping in the harbour.

But Matheson had his problems. The failure of the potato crop in 1845 led to famine conditions in the island for the next five years. To relieve his tenants in the four Parishes of Lewis he provided work in road building, erecting quays and draining moorland for agriculture, all in an effort to relieve the real distress in which the island folk had found themselves. All this might indicate Matheson, who was made a Baronet in 1850, was a benevolent landowner, which he was to a degree. The problem for the Lewis Estate lay in the manner in which the Estate Factor, Donald Munro, operated which eventually led to Munro being the most hated man in Lewis.

After Matheson's death in 1878, his widow, Lady Matheson ran the

Lews Castle, Stornoway. The foundation stone was laid in 1847 and the building was ready for occupation by 1852 but not before many structural defects were remedied, such as rainwater streaming through the bay windows. The cost of the castle was some £40,000, with a further £49,000 spent on creating the wooded policies extending some 600 acres (243 hectares)

OLIVER CROMWELL

It might come as a surprise to many that the Lord Protector of England should have had an interest in Lewis, but because of an incident created by Lord Seaforth, he ordered a punitive expedition to Lewis in 1653. The Commonwealth forces set themselves up in Stornoway, dismantled much of old Stornoway Castle and built fortifications in the area between South Beach, Point Street and James Street. Nothing of the English garrison remains, but a map still exists showing a layout of the barracks, storehouse and trenches. The original is in the care and keeping of Worcester College, Oxford University.

Today, Stornoway's main thoroughfare is called Cromwell Street. When and why it became so is a mystery and no records seem to exist to give the town's historians any clue. In the 1820s, the street was called Dempster Street and Oliver Street, the former name arising from the fact that the old Town House, now a café, was used as the town's courthouse, from which punishment was dispensed to wrongdoers. Oliver was Captain Oliver who for many years operated from a Customs cutter in the Minch waters to catch smugglers landing wines, brandy, silks and other contraband goods for their clients. He is remembered in Oliver's Brae, just outside Stornoway.

estate until she died in 1896, when Lewis passed to her nephew. His son put the island on the market in 1918 when it was bought by Lord Leverhulme, founder of Lever Brothers. Matheson Road in Stornoway is a reminder of an interesting chapter in Lewis history.

MOMENTS IN HISTORY

THE *IOLAIRE*

In the closing hours of 1918, many Lewis people were celebrating not only the end of the World War I, but looking forward with much anticipation to the return of those members of their families who had survived the European conflict. But fate was to intervene, to visit on the island community a tragedy which is still remembered after some eighty years.

Many returning soldiers and sailors were boarded on to HM Yacht *Iolaire* at Kyle of Lochalsh, once the embarkation point for Stornoway ferries. Early on 1 January 1919 the ship struck a reef just outside Stornoway harbour, known locally as the 'Beasts of Holm', and foundered. Of those on board the Iolaire 205 lost their lives with only 79 people being saved. Most of these owed their lives to the strength and courage of a man from Ness, John F. MacLeod, who jumped from the sinking ship with a heaving line and, with some difficulty, managed to swim ashore and allow men from the ship to make their way to safety.

The effect on the island of the loss of the *Iolaire* was profound, with the removal from the potential future of Lewis of so many of the young community. A memorial to commemorate the incident can be seen at Holm.

The other memorial to the sacrifice made by Lewis in the carnage of World War I is the War Memorial standing on a hill just outside Stornoway which has a view of all the four parishes of the island. It was formally opened in September 1924 by Lord Leverhulme, his last public act before he left Lewis for good. The building itself is one of the most impressive of its kind in Scotland. Some 1,151 names relate to the 1914–1918 war, including those who lost their lives in the *Iolaire* disaster.

Of a total of 6,712 serving Lewismen, some 17 per cent made the supreme sacrifice. Almost every fit man joined the forces early. If the ratio of those killed to the total population then is taken into account, the island paid twice as much in loss as the rest of the British Isles. In 1958 bronze plaques were unveiled to remember 376 names of Lewis men and women who lost their lives in World War II. The War Memorial can be viewed from outside the building. Internally it is in a neglected state.

THE *METAGAMA*

The leeching of so much of the island community's human resources following the loss of the *Iolaire* had an effect which was to be felt for many

years. A saviour of sorts appeared in 1918 when Lord Leverhulme purchased the Lewis Estate. His ambitious plans for the creation of an indus-
trialised island based on the town of Stornoway and the fishing potential
around the Western Isles seemed too good to be true. But the demand by
returning ex-Servicemen for a few acres to form a croft was to defeat him.
Elsewhere in the Highlands land settlement was taking place and it was
reasonable that this should also occur in Lewis. But Leverhulme was
opposed to this and the subsequent land raids on farms at Tong, Gress and
Coll brought matters to a head.

At the time Leverhulme was spending some £200,000 a year in Lewis.
This came to a halt in May 1920 when all his development operations were
stopped which resulted in considerable distress. Leverhulme eventually
pulled out of Lewis, an action which was to lead indirectly to the appearance of the Canadian Pacific Railway ship *Metagama* outside Stornoway
harbour, to take 300 Lewis emigrants to Canada. In the following year
other CPR ships, *Marloch* and *Canada*, left Stornoway with another 560
young men and women for the same destination. It is generally accepted
that this scale of blood-letting had a devastating effect on the island's
potential to recover from the depressing years of World War I, which had
already all but destroyed the herring fishing industry.

The Butt of Lewis lighthouse, which became automatic in 1998. Built in 1862, it was machine-gunned by a German plane in November 1940 but little damage was caused

5 THE CROFTING LANDSCAPE

THE CROFTING COMMUNITY in the Highlands and Islands of Scotland legally came into being with the passing of the Crofting (Scotland) Act in 1886. The pre-natal years which heralded the Act were both sore and bloody and led to often violent confrontations between the people who lived on the land and the military forces which the law of Scotland had insisted on using to evict tenants from their holdings. The fact that land raids occurred in the 1920s in Lewis and elsewhere, leading to the break-up of farms to create smaller land-holdings, was an indication, if such were needed, that the 1886 Act did not wholly satisfy the needs of those who fought for legal recognition as crofters.

The ownership of the land in the Highlands and Islands has always been a contentious issue. Before the nineteenth century, most of the land was in the possession of landowners, mainly the chiefs of the clans who had obtained their titles as rewards from the Scottish Crown, inter-marriage with other land-owing families, or by underhand tactics. Land was occupied in the main by tenants who had some allegiance to the clan chief, either through blood-lines or because they carried a common name. After the Battle of Culloden in 1746, the old system fell under the pressure of change. Land was sold in great parcels to newcomers as sporting estates and vast acres were cleared of people who were forced to migrate to occupy poorer ground or emigrate across the Atlantic in atrocious conditions, such as in the type of coffin ships which took the Irish people away from Ireland during the famine years of the last century.

The tenants on these new estates had no rights. They could be moved at the factor's whim. During the early years of the eighteenth century, tenants were placed under duress to gather kelp seaweed from the shores and burn it to produce an ash which was a valuable source material in the making of glass and other industrial products. Landowners made vast fortunes while the miserable cash earnings of the workers were absorbed in paying rents to the same landowners. When the demand for kelp ash fell through

A typical croft at Skigersta near Ness, Lewis. The croft house is on its own feu, surrounded by the expanse of the township's common grazing on which sheep are allowed to roam at will and which is also the source of peat for fuel

CROFTING

Acts of Parliament do not change things overnight and the 1886 Crofters Act was no exception, though it did confer the title of 'crofter' on those who had a claim to live on their land. The Act did not offer the real change that was desperately needed: the enablement of crofters to work their land into some useful degree of fertility and gain some advantage from improvements, such as the erection of outbuildings for animals. If such improvements were made it was the landlord who benefitted.

In 1955 a new Act was passed to enable crofters to gain more economic advantage from their efforts. But this only helped those with large crofts with fertile ground. In 1976 more legislation was introduced to give a crofter the right to buy his/her croft. One might have expected many to take advantage of this opportunity, but only 5 percent of crofters took up the offer. The majority of crofters preferred to exist under the protection of the 1955 Act, mainly because of the availability of agricultural subsidies which are a necessary part of the income generated by crofting.

In the past few years there have been moves to enable crofters to purchase a whole estate, to bring it into community ownership. This has occurred in Assynt, Skye and the Isle of Eigg in the Inner Hebrides. These purchases are being watched with interest, if only to see how combined effort can be used to gain social and economic advantages for the whole community.

the floor around 1820, the population was found to have risen to such numbers that the land itself could not support the large families which had become so dependent on the kelp for an income.

Thirty years later the potato blight introduced depression, poverty and starvation as virtual ghosts stalking the land for victims. It was not surprising that the ordinary people became infused with ideas which would lead to a degree of emancipation from their sorry state. Their aspirations became politicised, influenced by the Irish Land League which had been created out of the problems in Ireland and which was to have a profound influence in the Highlands and Islands, leading to the founding of the Highland Land Law Reform Association.

In Lewis a stone was thrown into the pool of troubled waters. This occurred in 1874 when the crofters of the island of Bernera confronted the Lewis Estate and went straight into the pages of Highland history with an incident which became known as the 'Bernera Riots'. By 1881 agitation to achieve official recognition of the plight of crofters had not only been politicised but reached such a pitch that the Government of the day acted to set up a Royal Commission, known as the Napier Commission. The fact that in the same year the Irish Land Act was passed was to be used as a marker for Highland objectives.

SIMPLE HOSTELS

These are operated by the Gatliff Hebridean Hostels Trust, a voluntary organisation with charitable status. The Crofter Hostels are independent of the Scottish Youth Hostel Association but have an adopted status. There are eight hostels throughout the Western Isles. Those in Lewis and Harris are at Garenin, West Lewis (NB 193 442), Stockinish, Harris (HG 136 910), Kershader, South Lochs, Lewis (NB 342 213), and at Rheingidale, Harris (NB 229 018). Address for contact: 30 Francis Street, Stornoway.

The members of the Napier Commission travelled round the Highlands and Islands holding meetings at which they took evidence which was so overwhelming that the Crofters' Act was passed in 1886. This Act gave the crofters security of tenure and certain rights relating to agricultural practice, grazing and housing. But there were many others who were left with no title, called squatters, and it was this class of landless people who were to create demands for land in the twentieth century. The crofters had other problems. Because they were only tenants, they could not raise funds upon their property in the same way as a feuar or owner could, nor could they benefit directly from any improvements they made on their crofts.

Over the years legislation has been introduced in a series of fits and starts to allow a crofter to purchase his own house site and acquire croft land, though that land remains under crofting tenure. The crofting estates in Lewis and Harris are mostly privately owned but are under crofting tenure which means that the landlord's interests are confined to fishing, shooting and mineral rights.

The present crofting landscape in Lewis and Harris is a product of socio-agrarian change. Most crofts seen as one goes round these islands are individually fenced off and consist of a small unit of land of about

The sleeping area of the black house at Arnol, Lewis. The box beds gave some degree of privacy in the cramped quarters of the house

5–10 acres (2–4 hectares), though there are even smaller land-holdings. Arable cultivation, though this has declined significantly in recent years, includes potatoes, turnips, cereals and grass for hay or silage. Sheep constitute the livestock which are allowed to roam the moorland at will (and sometimes presenting themselves as moving and unpredictable hazards on the roads). On some crofts can still be seen former 'black house' dwellings now used as storage facilities, or left as grass-covered footings.

The visible evidence of crofting settlement history can still be seen. The dwelling at Arnol, Lewis (NB 312 491), represents a type of building which was once common throughout the islands. It incorporates a house and byre and is based on a vernacular design which could be said to be a thousand years old. The house at Arnol was constructed as late as 1885 and combined the need to accommodate the family and their livestock, principally cattle.

In the village of Garenin, Carloway, Lewis, some old houses are being renovated for occupation. One (No. 5) has been turned into a Youth Hostel. In the same area are signs of an Iron Age fortification, the remains of old fields in Fivig Glen and what could be a Norse settlement at Liamashader, thus offering a panoramic view of an historic association which pushes time back at least one thousand years.

An interesting old settlement site can be seen at Bragar, Lewis (NB 2948), by the seashore between Loch Arnol and Loch Ordais. It is a fascinating monument to a former system of land use and nucleated communal living which can be easily compared with the present-day linear crofting townships of North and South Bragar.

The west coast of Harris, with its fertile machair lands, were once occupied by many crofters. But they were shifted to the rocky east coast and had to re-start their lives from almost bare ground. These townships are dotted along the road south from Tarbert to Rodel and cannot but raise one's admiration for the tenacity of those who remained on Harris rather than seek new lives across the Atlantic.

An extract from the writings of an observer, dated 1823, gives a graphic picture of the astonishing hardships which were experienced by islanders forcibly removed from their holdings to other parts of Lewis and Harris:

> The situation of the new lotters beggars description. It is worse than anything I saw in Donegal (Ireland) where I always considered human wretchedness to have reached the very acme. . . To erect their cabins, the sward was taken off the whole line of the intended road which has now become a morass, dangerous for both man and beast, to set their foot upon; how children contrive out and in their cabins baffles my comprehension, for the men have literally to step up to their knees in mud, the moment they quit their threshold.

MONUMENTS TO THE HEROES

IN RECENT YEARS the crofting landscape in Lewis has been provided with new stone-built monuments marking historic moments and events in the island which were significant in the gradual emergence of the crofting community to a legal status. These take various forms and can be seen at Balallan, Aignish and Gress. Bernera also has a fitting reminder of the events of 1874.

BERNERA

In April 1874, 150 crofters from the island of Bernera, along with others from Uig, marched to the door of Lews Castle in Stornoway to complain about the 56 families who had been served with eviction notices. They saw the owner of Lewis, Sir James Matheson, who placed full responsibility, like Pilate, on the shoulders of his factor, Donald Munro.

Though the crofters had been on a peaceful march to air their grievances, three men were later brought to trial, which, as fate would have it, was to herald a seminal change in the relationship between landlords and their tenants. Defended by a brilliant lawyer from Inverness, the accused

The atmospheric, if smoke-filled, interior of the black house at Arnol, Lewis. Built around 1885, this is a traditional drystone thatched house, typical of the vernacular architecture of the Western Isles in the nineteenth century

men were found not guilty, and the threatened eviction notices were withdrawn. In addition, the Lewis Estate factor, Munro, was removed from his position. The verdict was victory in the struggle of the crofters for recognition of their basic rights.

The 1874 event is now commemorated in a monument, in the form of a cairn, beside the bridge going over to the island.

BALALLAN

Just south of the township of Balallan, on the road to Harris, a cairn stands on a low hill, erected to commemorate the Park Deer Raid of November 1887. This district of South Lochs had suffered a great deal from evictions, extreme poverty and the fact that some 300 families were without land (they had been left out of the provisions of the 1886 Crofter Act) and squatting on other people's already over-burdened crofts. The main source of grievance was the fact that whole townships had been cleared to make way for the creation of a sporting estate.

Matters came to a head when a decision was made to call out men from all parts of North and South Lochs to gather at Balallan to prepare to raid Eishken Estate to shoot some deer. The authorities were informed of the intended raid. A few deer were shot to feed the raiding force of some 200 men. After two days the raiders returned home.

In the meantime the authorities had requested the presence on the island of Marines and they duly arrived in Stornoway. In this event a number of men were arrested and charged with mobbing, rioting and intimidation. The trial took place in Edinburgh but the men were found not guilty as libelled.

The memorial cairn at Balallan is now an interesting monument to the crofters' struggles for justice.

AIGNISH

In January 1888 a crowd of some 400 gathered at Aignish to protest against the presence of two farms, at Aignish and Melbost, which, they claimed, denied people of the Point district the necessary ground for more crofts in the area, particularly for those squatters who had been excluded under the terms of the 1886 Crofters Act.

Marines and Royal Scots soldiers, with policemen, confronted the crowd. The Riot Act was read but ignored. Scuffles broke out and a number of men were arrested and taken to Dingwall on the Scottish mainland before they went to Edinburgh for trial. Unlike those who

The peaceful graveyard at Bosta on the island of Great Bernera, Lewis, looking towards some islands at the entrance to Loch Roag

Top: The magnificent memorial cairn symbolising the meeting of Lord Leverhulme and the land raiders of Coll and Gress

Above: The memorial cairn, built in 1996, commemorating the Aignish Riot in 1888 when crofters from the Eye Peninsula agitated for more land to be given over to create crofts. They were confronted by the forces of law and the military. Thirteen crofters were arrested and sent for trial in Edinburgh and imprisoned. Seventeen years later the farm at Aignish was broken up and divided into crofts

had taken part in the Park Deer Raid, most received prison sentences. Thus the Aignish Riot entered the crowded pages of crofting history. The memorial monument at Aignish is designed to symbolise the confronting forces: law and order versus the cry for natural justice.

GRESS

The efforts of Lord Leverhulme to introduce developments based on industrialisation into the Lewis scene has been mentioned already. The demand for land by ex-servicemen returning from World War I was to introduce an element into his ambitions which eventually led him to leave Lewis and concentrate his ideas in Harris.

In March 1919 Leverhulme decided on a face-to-face meeting with those who agitated for a break-up of the farms at Tong, Coll and Gress. Over a thousand men and women gathered at Gress Bridge to hear Leverhulme state his case. He told them of his plans to spend over £5 million on a great fishing fleet, a large canning factory, light railways and an electric power station. There would be steady work for all, he said.

He was told that no person opposed his plans, but the land issue was important to them and their aim was to be given crofts and security of tenure. The matter was one of principle. In the event, the farms of Gress and Coll were raided and occupied, and Coll and Gress are now crofting communities. The memorial cairn at Gress, like that at Aignish, symbolises the historic meeting in 1919.

6 STORNOWAY – ISLAND CAPITAL

LONG BEFORE THE VIKINGS swept across the North Sea to invade the western seaboard of Scotland at the turn of the ninth century, the almost land-locked inner waters around what was to become Stornoway were considered by a much earlier people as a fitting place for settlement. Of all the ports on the deeply serrated west coast of Scotland, Stornoway had been blessed with one of the finest locations for a safe harbour. Set in the crook of an inner harbour and protected from the usually turbulent waters of the Minch by two effective land arms, the town is a natural haven for shipping. The presence of a chambered cairn (NB 417 323) on Gallows Hill overlooking the town suggests that for some time before the advent of the Iron Age the early inhabitants of Lewis recognised the value of the combined natural features. These latter included the relative fertility of the soils in the area, the shallow waters of Broad Bay, forming a perfect breeding ground for fish, freshwater rivers attractive to spawning salmon and sea-trout, and a safe and sheltered anchorage.

Little wonder then that by the time the Vikings arrived on the east coast of Lewis, rowing their longships into the bay, they named the place 'Steering Bay' in their Norse tongue, which eventually became the present-day Stornoway. There are, of course, no records of what native people the Vikings might have encountered. No doubt the settlement comprised rude huts occupied by simple farmers and fishermen who probably spoke a

The inner harbour at Stornoway

81

mixture of Gaelic and Pictish. Whether these people were left alone to their own devices, were put to the sword or enslaved, is a matter for conjecture.

What is certain is that, in the fullness of time, the Norsemen secured their control over Lewis and Harris and the rest of the Western Isles, their original visits, intent on plundering and looting, giving way to settlement and colonisation. The Norse period in the islands lasted to the middle of the thirteenth century, by which time ruling Norse-derived families (MacLeods, Morrisons, Nicolsons and MacAulays) had established themselves, no doubt inter-marrying with some of the local population. The main legacy of the Vikings in Lewis and Harris still exists in the vast number of Norse-based place-names around the coasts of the islands, and the

love of the sea inborn in many islanders as later history was to prove. But of the physical remains of the Norsemen, there is surprisingly little, though some sites are now being identified by excavation and the findings as yet open to scholarly interpretation.

By the time the Norse finally left Lewis, under the terms of the Treaty of Perth (1266), all Norway's possessions on the western seaboard of Scotland were ceded to King Alexander III of Scotland. In the power vacuum left by the Norse kinglets, other political and territorial aspirants moved in to fill the space. Although legally the Western Isles were subject to a Scottish king during the fourteenth century they fell under the authority of the Lordship of the Isles, a Gaelic–speaking political entity which

A panoramic view of Stornoway from Gallows Hill. The nearby Neolithic chambered cairn, now somewhat obscured by a modern cairn, is an indication that long before the Vikings arrived the site was of strategic importance, given the wide views of the area

had sufficient clout to enable it to sign treaties with England without reference to the King of Scotland. During the period of the Lordship, 1354 to 1493, clan leaders strengthened their control over their local territory. Lewis, by the end of the fourteenth century, was held by one branch of the clan MacLeod, with Harris being controlled from Skye by another branch of the same clan.

So far as Stornoway was concerned, by the fifteenth century it boasted the Castle of Stornoway which reflected something of the architectural style of Kismul Castle at Castlebay in Barra. For the Lewis MacLeods, the castle was an essential symbol of power and status and was thus the natural target of punitive expeditions sent by the Scottish Parliament in Edinburgh in attempts to curb the independence of the unruly clan MacLeod. The castle was attacked in 1506 and again in 1554 but survived siege and bombardment until its fate was eventually sealed when Stornoway was occupied by forces of Cromwell's Commonwealth, who caused the structure to be 'broken down'. Thereafter the ruins remained as a silent witness to the MacLeods' once powerful hold on Lewis, until 1882 when the site was demolished and overtaken by improvements to Stornoway Harbour. A plaque on the Maritime Building on No.1 Pier is now the only sign that a castle once stood on the town's foreshore.

The Sir Max Aitken lying at anchor in Stornoway Harbour. The first lifeboat which arrived in Stornoway was the Isabella in 1897. Since then Stornoway has been the base for the life-saving craft serving the Minch area. Much of the rescue activities are now carried out by the helicopter air-sea rescue services

No doubt the presence of the original castle on Stornoway's South Beach acted as a catalyst for the town's early beginnings. It is thought that the earliest settlement was arranged along the spine of a natural low-lying promontory, now called Point Street, with parallel developments on North Beach and South Beach. The latter still has its small stretch of sea-washed sand, perhaps somewhat a little nervous and incongruous among the present harbour facilities worth some £60 million and fated, sometime in the future, to be concreted over to erase the last visual element of some one thousand years of local history.

With the castle as a community focal point, the town came of age in 1607 with its elevation into a Burgh of Barony, though it obviously had some commercial importance before that date for it to become eligible for Burgh status. By rights Stornoway should have been made a Royal Burgh, but opposition from such other Burghs as Inverness and Dingwall on the Scottish mainland, who thought their own commercial advantages in the north of Scotland would suffer, put paid to Stornoway's ambition.

The Burgh Charter was granted by King James VI to one of the men who was involved in a colonising scheme to bring some degree of civilisation to Lewis. This scheme embraced a group of speculative entrepreneurs from Fife, known in island history as the Fife Adventurers. They landed in Stornoway in 1598 with the express purpose of exploiting the agricultural and fishing potential of Lewis. In fact, they were sold short: Lewis was hardly a land flowing with milk and honey, nor was it the El Dorado they were told it was. In addition they reckoned without the violent opposition of the Lewis MacLeods who thwarted their every endeavour. In the end the disappointed Fife Adventurers left Lewis, with the vacuum filled by the scheming Mackenzie of Kintail who not only had his own eye upon Lewis but who had contrived the failure of the colonising scheme. He gained Lewis for himself in 1610, with Stornoway a worthwhile speculative property. The Charter reads:

> And we give grant to the present inhabitants of the said burgh, full and free power and liberty of buying and selling within the burgh of the same wine, wax, cloth both broad and narrow, garments coloured and shorn, cheap and dear, along with all other merchandise. And the power and liberty of holding and having within the said burgh bakers, brewers, sellers of whisky, butchers, fishers and all other craftsmen pertaining to a free burgh.

Under the new owner of Lewis, eventually to be raised to the status of Lord Seaforth, Stornoway was developed with the town becoming an important port, not only for general shipping but for the shipping industry, to assist with which Seaforth imported Dutch fishermen to organise the fisheries in the waters of the Minch.

Seaforth built a substantial house for himself, Seaforth Lodge, on a site now occupied by Lews Castle (built c 1850). Of passing interest is Seaforth's allegiance to the Jacobite cause and his use of Seaforth Lodge to accommodate the planners of the ill-fated 1719 Jacobite Rising. Another passing indication of Stornoway's political importance is the historical fact that the town was the meeting place for emissaries of England and Sweden, whose respective countries, in Queen Elizabeth's reign, plotted against the Scottish Crown to gain mutually beneficial advantages.

Stornoway was regarded as being of sufficient strategic importance to the army of Oliver Cromwell's Commonwealth in that it secured defences in Lewis by building fortified barracks and supporting warehouses in the Point Street area of the town. Today, Stornoway's main thoroughfare is called Cromwell Street, for some mysterious and obscure reason, though it had other names in the past.

COMING OF AGE

BY THE END OF the eighteenth century, Stornoway was looking good as a town of commercial substance. An oil painting, executed in 1798, had as its subject the many substantial slated houses gracing North Beach, South Beach and what is now called Cromwell Street, all proving that the town had grown in status, as had the commercial, industrial and social sectors of the burgh. The painting is thought to have been commissioned by the

ST PETER'S, STORNOWAY

This church was built in 1839 and, along with St Molouadh's at Eoropie, Ness, Lewis, serves the congregation of the Scottish Episcopal Church in Lewis. The ceiling of the building has ornate plasterwork. The octagonal pulpit was originally in King's College, London, and bears carved figures. The church bell originally belonged to the Old Parish Church in Stornoway, St Lennan's, now disappeared from its site on North Beach Street. Of Dutch origin, it bears the date 1631. In the church's care and keeping are the Prayer Book of David Livingstone, the African missionary, and a copy of the 1608 'Breeches Bible', wherein the word 'breeches' in Genesis Chapter 3, is substituted for 'aprons'.

The vessel Greenpeace berthed at Stornoway Harbour, a common sight in 1997 after spells at sea monitoring the explorations for new oil fields in the North Atlantic

proprietor of Lewis who, in 1797, was created Lord Seaforth, Baron Mackenzie of Kintail and appointed Governor of Barbados, a post he held from 1800 to 1806. No doubt the painting was something of a celebratory commission to provide an after-dinner talking point.

By 1821 a map of the town revealed that Stornoway was expanding, with a number of main streets laid out on a grid plan with the urban area encroaching on two small villages, Bayhead and Newton, both of which are still remembered in their street names and are now part of greater Stornoway.

The character of town life was also changing, with the citizens aspiring to create the trappings of successful society. In 1756 the Post Office opened its first official presence in the Western Isles. In 1765 a Customs House was established, indicating that the amount of shipping between Europe and the Americas was significant and a potential source of revenue for the Crown. In 1767 the Masonic brethren got together to establish Fortrose Lodge, now the oldest private institution in the town. Its archives contain some of Stornoway's most valuable historic records, silent witnesses to the extensive activity once seen in the busy harbour. The names of the captains, officers and crewmen appear in the Lodge register, associated with barques, brigs, schooners and full-rigged ships from ports ranging from Amsterdam, Danzig, Trondheim, Copenhagen, Stavanger, Hamburg and Jersey, in addition to such home ports as Liverpool, Hull, London, Newcastle, Aberdeen and Greenock. Stornoway had in fact become a cosmopolitan crossroads which, in turn, inspired many Lewismen to go to sea for a career, from deck-hands to captains.

Family names such as MacDonald, Ryrie, Morrison and Mackenzie were to be found as captains and skippers of some of the best-known sailing ships on the seven seas of the last century, like the *Sir Launcelot*, the *Assaye* and other fast clippers, even the Aberdeen-built *Stornoway*, which brought tea from China and wool from New Zealand to the lucrative London markets.

While Stornoway's association with the world's oceans was by proxy, the connection with the seas round the Western Isles was perhaps stronger, for it was the rich waters of the Minch which laid the foundations for the town's prosperity. Not for nothing did the coat of arms of the now defunct Stornoway Burgh include three fish emblazoned on the shield over the motto: 'God's Providence is our Inheritance'.

THE FIRST CUNARDER

In 1847 the first ship of the newly formed Cunard Line (whose partners included the MacIver family from Lewis) to sail into New York was the Hibernia, *captained by Alick Ryrie from Stornoway. The captain of the finest clipper ever built, the* Sir Launcelot, *was a Lewis man, Murdo Stewart MacDonald. The island connection with the Cunard Line was maintained in this century when the late Donald MacLean became Commodore Captain of the company.*

BOOM YEARS

WHEN THE HERRING FISHING took off in earnest in the middle of the last century, Stornoway thrived in the exciting air of trade and commerce brought by the herring boom. The town was recognised as a major European fishing port, exporting herring to Russia, the Baltic ports,

Germany and Spain. One can imagine a young Stornoway lad walking down Cromwell Street, brushing past Norwegians, Frenchmen, Russians and the local captains home on leave from voyages round the world, all of whom must have added an element of virtual reality to a geography lesson in the town's school, the Nicolson Institute.

In 1918, the island of Lewis was bought by Lord Leverhulme, who had created the Sunlight soap company, now called Unilever. He had plans to make Stornoway the fishing capital of the world, based on a large ocean-going fleet of fishing vessels and an industrial canning and processing complex in the town. But his far-sighted ambitions were frustrated by the demands from returning World War I ex-servicemen in Lewis who wanted a few acres of land to create their own crofts, which had been promised them by the British Government as part of the idea that the country could become 'a land fit for heroes'.

A lesser man would have pulled out of Lewis in a fit of pique but Leverhulme was not of that mould. Before he put Lewis on the market he gifted in perpetuity to the citizens of Stornoway a vast estate of crofting moorland and crofting townships, Lews Castle and its wooded policies. The gift, set up in 1923, is today administered by the Stornoway Trust on behalf of the townspeople. Until recently, the Trust was unique in being the only body of its kind in Britain with its lands in community ownership.

Stornoway Town Hall, now an art gallery. The first structure was opened in 1905 but burnt down in 1918. The restored building was re-opened in 1929

Opposite: A careful eye on one of the putting greens at Stornoway Golf Course, an 18-hole course which attracts many golfers looking for a challenge to their skills during the summer Open Competitions

Below: The Lewis War Memorial just outside Stornoway. It was opened by Lord Leverhulme in 1924. Its location on a low hill was chosen because all four Lewis Parishes can be seen on a clear day. Inside are two moulded panels containing the names of 1,151 Lewismen killed in World War I

THE ARCHITECTURAL HERITAGE

DUE TO THE ERADICATION of much of the town's older buildings in the 1950s and 1960s, Stornoway today hardly reflects the interesting and characteristic community it once was. Even so, there are architectural echoes of its past built heritage. One area which reflects something of former times is on North Beach Street, near the old sail loft (c 1830) and the Lewis Hotel, bearing the date 1829. This part of the town still retains an architectural integrity which, with little imagination, could be restored to provide a solid and visible link with a lively and interesting past.

There are also buildings which echo Georgian architecture, such as the Town House which predates 1821, and the Victorian excessive aspirations to grandeur embodied in the Town Hall, opened in 1905 and restored in 1929 after a disastrous fire. The houses on James Street (c 1890) are evidence of the wealth created by the herring fishing industry. Matheson Road and Anderson Road are interesting if only because of the building styles of the houses, with the latter reflecting their English garden-city styles, one visible legacy of Lord Leverhulme's pervading influence.

Throughout the town there are structures which serve as historical punctuation marks in the development of Stornoway. The Masonic Lodge on Kenneth Street (1822) is unassuming in itself but was in its time a focal point for many of the community's social activities. On Keith Street is the somewhat darkly forbidding Female Industrial School (1848) built by Lady Matheson to give girls the necessary education in those domestic activities thought necessary to prepare them for their adult lives. The awkward and rather incongruous clock tower, rising from the more modern and stark complex of the Sports Centre, is a remaining part of the original Nicolson Institute opened in 1873.

The former lively commercial activity of Stornoway is reflected in the bank buildings, with the earliest dated 1868. Their substantial construction, relieved by ornate decoration, exuded the necessary confidence needed by customers concerned for the safety of their hard-earned cash.

It is, however, Lews Castle which is the town's pride and joy, though its current dilapidated state is a matter for some community concern. When Sir James Matheson bought Lewis in 1844 he decided to have a palatial residence in Stornoway. With this in mind he razed to the ground the former Seaforth Lodge, and the castle's foundation stone was laid, with full Masonic honours, in November 1847. The building was ready for occupation in 1852. It was furnished with many luxurious features, such as carved wood panelling and tapestries from the Gobelin factories in France. Crystal chandeliers gave an extra glitter to social occasions. All these were removed by Lord Leverhulme after he bought Lewis in 1917.

Today, Stornoway exudes a lively atmosphere, acting as it does as a communal focal point for industry, commerce and administration, and, be it said, the main shopping centre for the population in the Lewis hinter-

Opposite: The popular golf course at Scarista, Harris, where it is sometimes difficult to concentrate on the ball with so much spectacular scenery to divert the eye

Below: An Lanntair, Stornoway's innovative art and events gallery. The picture on the left shows Iain Brady's mixed media sculpture for an exhibition entitled 'Singing the Fishing'

land. The town's leisure provisions, for locals and visitors alike, are as comprehensive as one might find in any town or city aware of the need for people to relax from the stresses of the world of work. Stornoway Golf Club and Sea Angling Club both cater for specialist sports pursuits. The former mounts a series of Open Golf competitions during the summer months and in 1997 opened a fully comprehensive Club House. The Sea Angling Club, some of whose members are now the wearers of Scotland caps for Scottish and International angling competitions, has built up a reputation for its highly efficient Open Angling Competitions which attract both British and Continental visitors.

The Lewis Sports Centre, based in the town, offers a wide range of activities from swimming to fitness gyms. There are clubs devoted to canoeing, running, freshwater angling (brown and rainbow trout), with visitors being offered moor trekking, horse-riding, nature trails, sea trips and croft-related holidays where one can participate in the day-to-day working on crofts and pick up a few useful words of Gaelic in the process.

On the right is part of the exhibition 'Tir nan Og – The Life and Times of Angus Og'. Angus Og was a cartoon creation of Ewan Bain who for many years contributed the cartoon strip in the Scottish Daily Record *(Photographs courtesy of Sam Maynard)*

Of a more leisurely nature but with an intellectual content, the award-winning art gallery, An Lanntair, on South Beach has a continually changing programme of exhibitions of photographs, paintings and sculptures, including events devoted to the interpretation of the cultural heritage of the islands. History is also on show at Museum nan Eilean on Francis Street while those of a more literary mind can indulge in the excellent local reference section in the Public Library on Keith Street.

During the summer months car parking can be a bit of a headache in the town, but it is not an insurmountable problem if one takes the advice of the staff at the Tourist Office on Cromwell Street.

Visitors will have some piece of mind should any emergency crop up during a visit. The recently opened £30 million Western Isles Hospital provides medical facilities, a far cry from 1795 when there was only one doctor to cover the whole of Lewis – and he was based in Stornoway.

7 A HARRIS VIGNETTE

HARRIS IS A PLACE of astonishing contrasts. In the north there are mountains reaching an honourable height in the Clisham at 2,293ft (699m). They are interesting from a geological viewpoint because they projected above the 2,000ft (610m) thickness of the ice-sheet which covered most of the Western Isles about 10,000 years ago. Then there are fertile machairs on the west coast fringed with broad, sandy beaches. This area once housed most of the population of Harris up until the end of the eighteenth century when the people were cleared to make way for sheep farms. Some emigrated to Cape Breton; others elected to stay in Harris and moved to the east side of Harris to what is now called the Bays area.

The coast along the south of Harris overlooks yet another vista – the islands in the Sound of Harris. These range from rocky reefs which dry out at low water offering a resting place for gannets and other sea-birds, to large islands which once bore a healthy population until they, too, were cleared. Some of the more inaccessible islands, like Shillay, in the western approaches to the Sound, are home to breeding colonies of seals.

A welcome from Postman Pat to the Post Office at Northton, Harris, one of the many highland community essential facilities serving the scattered townships

91

The remote western side of North Harris, at Hushinish where the road peters out and the next stop is America

On the east coast of Harris lie a string of townships created last century by the people evicted from the west coast. What is seen today is the result of years of making the most of what could be used in terms of thin soil for planting of potato beds in 'lazybeds' – literally thin strips of piled-up earth. Fortunately the rocky shores yielded up a sufficient harvest of fish and shellfish to keep body and soul together until houses could be built and crofts established.

The interior of Harris has been called a moonscape, with large tracts of bare rock which have been exposed to wind and rain for thousands of years, to little effect for the gneiss is a hard, unyielding material and contributes little to the making of soils. But some soil does exist in isolated pockets: the deposits of till or boulder clay which were laid down as the ice-sheets moved to grind the rocks down to particle size, but often leaving huge boulders high and dry on the tops of high places. There are some spectacular perched blocks near Manish School (NG 109 895) which look as though they might have been placed there by someone with a droll sense of humour.

HISTORY

THE MACLEODS OF HARRIS came originally from the same Norse stock as the MacLeods of Lewis, through Tormod (Norman) the son of Leod; his brother Thorcuil (Torquil) got Lewis as his possession. The earliest Charter given to the MacLeods of Harris, by David II of Scotland, is dated 1343. In 1498, a descendant, Alastair Crotach MacLeod, received a charter from King James IV and seemingly was a trusted friend of the King. It was this Alastair who restored St Clement's Church at Rodel and had a tomb built for himself in 1528, though he was not to die until some twenty years later.

At the time of the 1745 Jacobite Rising, the Chief of the Harris MacLeods, Norman, was a waster who spent his money and resources on gambling which he tried to recoup by raising the rents of his tenants, a burden they could ill afford. In 1772 his grandson inherited both property and his grandfather's debts, which amounted to, at that time, something in the region of £50,000. He was General Sir Norman MacLeod who, in an effort to clear the debts, sold Harris and St Kilda to Captain Alexander MacLeod for £15,000.

Captain MacLeod had made his fortune from his ship *The Lord Mansfield*, trading for the East India Company, and decided to use his new property as an arena for commercial opportunities. He encouraged the Harris fishing industry and improved harbour facilities. He set up a factory for spinning woollen and cotton thread and twine for herring nets. He brought from Scotland's east coast fishermen, Orkney-designed yawls to teach locals how to exploit the herring fishing. And he advanced money for the purchase of boats, built cottages for families and generally improved the lot of his tenants. At Rodel he built a house for himself alongside a new pier and harbour. In addition, he spent money in the restoration of St Clement's Church at Rodel in 1787.

But by 1834 the Harris estate had gone on to the market. Captain MacLeod's grandson sold the property to the Earl of Dunmore. He in turn sold North Harris to Sir Edward Scott

There is a bit of wind on most days in the islands. Here the wind coming off Loch Seaforth is being put to good use

in 1868, now remembered in the name of the secondary school in Tarbert. From then on Harris saw a number of owners, each of whom has made some impact on the countryside.

TARBERT

TARBERT IS THE CENTRAL village in Harris and is the ferry terminal connecting Uig on Skye and Lochmaddy on North Uist. Shops, hotels and other facilities have good standards of service and cater for most needs of the population of North Harris within reasonable travelling distance. Its streets hoist themselves up steep inclines and run down braes, all of which require careful driving. Access to and from the ferry terminal is now much better than the old days when the town was log-jammed with traffic at ferry berthing and boarding times. The local Tourist Office on the road down to the pier is well staffed and stocked to provide information on Harris, backed up by a plentiful supply of booklets and leaflets on subjects relating to Harris. A display of local history is usually provided in the old school hostel.

The impressive Scottish baronial pile of Amhuinnsuidhe Castle, Harris. Built in 1868 as the Harris seat of the Earl of Dunmore, who bought Harris in 1834, it was originally called Fincastle. It has seen a number of owners and tenants. The latter include Thomas Sopwith, the aircraft pioneer who built the aeroplane which was used in the first attempt to cross the Atlantic

Oppostie: The sea inlet of Geo Martin, at Horgabost, Harris, on a day when the Atlantic shows its ill temper

Right: Weaving tweed on the Hattersley loom, introduced to the islands by Lord Leverhulme in the 1920s. Here, the weaving at Plocrapool, Harris, is producing the more traditional, heavy-weight cloth with a hand-crafted cachet

Inspecting the dyed wool at the Soay Studio, Harris, part of the many processes which go to make Harris Tweed

HARRIS TWEED

IN 1842, SO THE story goes, the Countess of Dunmore, whose family had bought Harris in 1834, purchased a length of tweed cloth. The quality of the weaving so impressed her that she decided to promote the cloth by, first, sending Harris girls to Paisley to get proper training and then encouraging others to take up production of the tweed. In a handful of years the fame of the cloth became widely known and started off what is now the Harris Tweed industry. At the present time the centre of the industry is in Lewis and the Harris contribution, per se, is small. There are, however, a number of Harris Tweed weavers in Harris who still produce the heavier, more traditional weights of cloth, eagerly sought by those who prefer the hand-crafted product.

During the summer months, a Harris Tweed and local history exhibition is on display at the school in Drinishader. Other places offering an insight into the traditional and modern methods of the production of tweed include Leverburgh (at An Clachan), Liceasto (wooden loom weaving and natural dyes), Plocropol and Luskentyre.

LORD LEVERHULME

AFTER LORD LEVERHULME gave up on his development plans for Lewis, he focused his attention on Harris. In 1919 he purchased North Harris from

Sir Samuel Scott for £20,000 and, concurrently with his schemes for Lewis, sketched out some ideas which he hoped would benefit Harris. One of his projects was based at Bunabhuinneader, near Ardhasaig. This was a whaling station which had been established in the 1890s to catch whales in the Atlantic. Leverhulme bought out the Norwegian interests in the facility and for a time the station was producing whale oil and meat for the African markets. But the enterprise failed and today the only relic of the former activity is the high chimney of the dessicating plant.

Leverhulme's main interest centred on the small village of Obbe (Gaelic: An t-Ob), renamed Leverburgh in 1923. He tried to transform the place into a big fishing port, building piers, jetties, roads and houses and blasting away many of the rocks which prevented easy access to the harbour. The project was abandoned in 1925 when Leverhulme died. The harbour installations which originally cost £250,000 were sold for £5,000 to a demolition company. A few of the original buildings can still be seen.

Leverburgh is the ferry terminal for crossing over the Sound of Harris to Otternish, North Uist (one hour), from where another ferry takes locals and visitors onto the island of Berneray. At the time of writing a causeway is being constructed between the island and North Uist.

SCARP ISLAND

THE ROAD TO THE now-deserted island of Scarp turns right at the bottom of the Clisham, past the remnants of the old whaling station and westwards to Hushinish, following a circuitous route along the northern shore of Loch Tarbert. Here, there is a magnificent sandy beach and, nearby, the old jetty which was once used to provide access to Scarp. The island was deserted by its population in 1971. It has an interesting claim to a niche in postal history. In July 1934 it was the location for one of three British rocket-mail experiments, suggested by the inventor of a rocket, Herr Zucker, who was later to become prominent in V-rocket work during World War II.

The first rocket was fired from Scarp to the Harris mainland but it exploded prematurely and most of the mail was damaged. Then the mail was jetted across the water in a second firing. The whole experiment, however, was deemed a failure. The route taken by the mail items addressed to Kirkwall, Orkney, was unique: rocket, ferry-boat, motor car, mail steamer, railway train and, finally, by Highland Airways to Kirkwall.

SCALPAY ISLAND

UP UNTIL 1997, SCALPAY, on the east side of Harris, was actually an island. It is now accessed by a road bridge. Unlike the island of Scarp, Scalpay has managed to maintain its population, not because of the fertility

The imposing Borve Lodge, Harris, once used by Lord Leverhulme as his headquarters when he was developing nearby Leverburgh into a major fishing port. Close by the Lodge are the ruins of a dun or broch and in the vicinity are three rocks with carved depressions known as cup-marks

The deserted island of Scarp off the west coast of Harris. The last of its population left in 1971. In 1934 the island was the scene of an experiment to send mail by rocket. The rocket exploded and the idea was pronounced a failure. Today some of the fire-damaged postal items are worth a few hundred pounds to collectors

of the ground but because its economy was based on fishing. At one time Scalpay had the largest number of fishermen employed, outside of Stornoway, and worked a total of 33 boats. In addition, native enterprise established a ship-owning firm whose vessels carried freight and passengers to many parts of Scotland and, on occasion, to the Continent. Today the fishing is concentrated on prawns, lobsters and other shellfish.

At the eastern end of the island is Eilean Glas Lighthouse, the first ever sea-warning facility to be erected in the Western Isles, in 1789, though an earlier start on the site had been made by the enterprising Captain MacLeod of Harris. It is now an automated light.

ST CLEMENT'S, RODEL

THIS BUILDING HAS JUSTLY been described as an ecclesiastical jewel. Certainly it is the most impressive structure of its kind on the west of Scotland. Built on the site of a much older religious settlement, the church as it stands today represents the work of Alastair Crotach (Hunchback) MacLeod of Harris in the 1520s. While the outside of the building is impressive, the interior of the church is quite stunning, in particular the carved wall tombs. They represent what is judged to be the finest ensemble of late medieval sculpture to survive anywhere in the Western Isles. The other wall tomb in St Clement's is that of William MacLeod, son of Alastair Crotach who died in 1551.

The church tower is built on an outcrop of rock, at a higher level than the rest of the church. There are several carved panels, facing the four cardinal points, one of which has the figure of a bishop, perhaps St Clement himself. It is supposed that Clement was the third Bishop of Rome after St Peter, and was much favoured as a patron of churches in the medieval Norse world. This might account for the size of the whole building, by Hebridean standards. Only the Benedictine abbey on Iona is larger.

St Clement's is normally open all year to visitors but if it is closed the key can be obtained from nearby Rodel Hotel bar.

Overleaf: The ecclesiastical jewel of the Outer Hebrides. St Clement's Church at Rodel is reckoned to be a site which goes back some 1,500 years. The building exudes the very atmosphere of island history
Inset: A disc-headed cross made from black schist depicting the Crucifixion, in St Clement's Church, Rodel, Harris

Grave slabs in St Clement's Church, Rodel, Harris. They are heavily ornamented with sword designs and interlaced panels. Four of them were originally in the floor of the church choir. They date from the fifteenth and early sixteenth centuries. The fifth (extreme right) is dated 1725, and the initials probably stand for Roderick Campbell and his wife Ann MacSween. Campbell may have been a former Chamberlain of Harris

8 OUT AND ABOUT

I T IS NOT PROPOSED here to offer routes for walking or to provide information for car outings. The local Tourist Board has been innovative in producing a series of cheap pamphlets (50p each at the time of writing) which detail walks of moderate category which can be undertaken to allow the visitor to 'home in' on the detail in a small area of Lewis or Harris. To date these walks include Calanais, Tolsta to Ness, Rheinigidale in Harris and Stockinish also in Harris. These walks are designed to highlight wildlife, historical and prehistoric sites and something of the geological make-up of the islands.

Many visitors tend to be unaware of the fairly long distances which can be travelled in Lewis and Harris. For example, with Stornoway as a starting point, Ness is some 28 miles (73km) away (45 minutes); Tarbert is 34 miles (88km) (under an hour); and Leverburgh is 55 miles (144km) (allow 1¹/₂ hours). Because of this it is essential to think in terms of a whole day for each district in order to get the most out of each trip, to view points of interest and some, at least, of the many scenic vista which catch the eye.

Maps are, of course, a useful source of detailed information, with the Ordnance Survey Pathfinder series covering all of Lewis and Harris (1:25000). These are ideal for the dedicated explorer intent on making personal in-depth discoveries. For those who simply wish to access more general but still comprehensive information the O.S. Landranger maps are recommended (1:50000).

Rush hour on the west coast of Harris. Here, Traigh Seilebost stretches almost to the horizon, one of many white sand beaches which are typical of the Atlantic coastal areas of the Western Isles

Overleaf: The Butt of Lewis lighthouse. Built in 1862, it became unmanned, or automatic in 1998. The lighthouse contains the automatic equipment for the operation of the lighthouse on the Flannan Isles, some 35 miles (89km) out in the Atlantic to the west

THE CROFTING CODE

In the islands there is a Crofting Code to be followed. Many areas are in the nature of working ground for crofters, even on the open moorland and hills. The following 'ground' rules have been devised in the interest of all who use the countryside:

- *Avoid damaging crops in the growing season in the crofting townships.*
- *Never leave gates open, to avoid the possibility of livestock wandering.*
- *Keep dogs under control at all times and on a leash, particularly where livestock may be near at hand.*
- *Cars should be parked where they will not cause a problem for others.*
- *Respect both historical and ancient monuments; they are the visible heritage of the islands.*
- *Protect wildlife and plants, particularly breeding birds.*

ACCESS

AS A GENERAL RULE most of Lewis and Harris can be accessed by the public but there are times in the year when estates indulge in shooting over the ground. At these times it is best to access local information, to be informed of restrictions which might be in force.

WEATHER AND WALKS

IT GOES WITHOUT SAYING that the weather in the islands can be changeable. May and June are generally sunny with dry weather between May and August. Days without some wind are rare so there is always the chance that a combination of wind and sun might require some application of protective creams. A lightweight waterproof is often a useful piece of wear. If going on some of the walks, strong and waterproof boots are advisable. Prevailing winds in Lewis and Harris tend to be southerly and south-westerly. Be advised that when in the higher hills the weather can change quickly and often without warning. And remember to leave information with someone on your estimated time of arrival after a jaunt out exploring the island.

Catching sight of sea-birds on the wing at the Butt of Lewis – a favourite place for birdwatchers
Opposite: Looking south down along the long stretch of Loch Seaforth, with Seaforth Island on the left

USEFUL INFORMATION AND PLACES TO VISIT

TOURIST INFORMATION CENTRES

Tourist Office: 26 Cromwell Street,
Stornoway, Lewis HS1 2DD
Tel: 01851 703088; Fax: 01851 705244.
Open all year.

Tourist Office: Pier Road, Tarbet, Harris.
Tel: 01859 502011.
Open early April to mid October.

FERRY/AIR SERVICES

Caledonian MacBrayne
Head Office:
The Ferry Terminal, Gourock PA19 1QP.
Tel: 08705 650000; Fax 01475 635235.

Local Offices:
Ferry Terminal, Stornoway, Lewis.
Tel: 01851 702361; Fax: 01851 705523

Tarbert, Harris.
Tel: 01859 502444; Fax: 01859 502017.

British Airways
Stornoway Airport.
Tel: 01851 703673.

PLACES TO VISIT

Arnol Black House, Arnol, Lewis
Traditional croft house and museum.

Borgh Pottery, Fivepenny House, Borve, Lewis
Hand-thrown stoneware pottery.

Ness Museum, Habost, Ness, Lewis
Local history display (open during summer months).

Calanais Visitor Centre, Callanish, Lewis
Interpretive Centre for the Callanish Stones;
shop and café.

Carloway Broch, Doune, Carloway, Lewis
Iron Age broch, viewing all year; Interpretive Centre.

Bernera Centre, Great Bernera, Lewis
Local history display, refreshments.
Open Easter to September.

Mrs K. Campbell, Plocrapool, Harris, at her Hattersley loom,
producing the world-famous Harris Tweed

Gearrannan 'Black House' Village, No. 3 Garenin,
Carloway, Lewis
Restoration of black houses.

Lochcroistean Centre, Uig, Lewis
Visitor centre with local history display, refreshments.
Open June to September.

Harris Tweed Mill, North Shawbost, Lewis
Guided tours of the mill.

Oiseval Gallery, Brue, Lewis
Creative landscape photography.

Morven Gallery, Barvas, Lewis
Paintings and sculptures, studio café.
Open April to September.

Coll Pottery, Back, Lewis
Pottery, crafts, pottery demonstrations, tea-rooms.

An Lanntair, Kenneth Street, Stornoway
Art centre (monthly exhibitions and has an
events programme), shop, café, bar and restaurant.

Lewis Loom Centre, Old Grainstore, Bayhead Street,
Stornoway.
Guided tour of Harris Tweed, weaving demonstrations.

Stornoway Sea Angling Club, Shell Street, Stornoway
Sea angling activities, competitions and club.

St. Columba's, Aignish, Lewis
Ruin of early church and ancient graveyard of
MacLeods of Lewis.

Co Leis Thu?, The Old Schoolhouse, Northton, Harris
Genealogical research centre and islands exhibition.

Borvemor Studios, 9 Scaristavore, Harris
Exhibitions, events, workshops and café.

Clachan, Leverburgh, Harris
Various island-related exhibitions, café and craft shop.

Bosta, the island of Great Bernera, Lewis. Here one can see the 'footprints' of an Iron Age settlement, where the outlines of a number of houses are preserved for posterity

St Clement's Church, Rodel, Harris
Outstanding church building with sculptured tomb.

Museum nan Eilean, Francis Street, Stornoway
Displays on local and island history.

Sports Centre, Sandwick Road, Stornoway
Swimming, sauna and gymnasium.

Stornoway Trust Ranger Services, Perceval Square, Stornoway

Provide guided tours around Stornoway and Castle grounds.

Public Library, Keith Street, Stornoway
Local history collections and reference centre.

Stornoway Golf Club, Willowglen Road, Stornoway
18-hole golf course and club.

Stornoway Bowling Club, Bayhead Street, Stornoway
Bowling green and club.

PLACE-NAMES AND THEIR MEANINGS

IT IS OFTEN SAID that the study of place-names and their meanings is a minefield for amateurs; in addition to a working knowledge of the languages involved, and the old versions at that (Old Norse and Gaelic where Lewis and Harris are concerned), there is also a need to be very familiar with the topography of an area. One major problem is the lack of documents in which the early forms of names in the islands appear, which would give interpreters a fair chance on deriving the original meaning of a place-name. Norse names were given to places when they arrived in the Western Isles c AD800. Whether these same places had names given to them by the earlier Celtic/Gaelic population and then were superimposed by Norse is speculation but may be a reasonable assumption.

In Gaelic, Lewis is Eilean Leodhais, which has a superficial likeness to the Norse Ljodhus. Early forms of the name are: Leodus (1150), Lodoux (1292), Leogas (1449) and Leoghais (1700). Around 1700, Martin Martin explained leog as 'water lying on the surface of the ground'. With more than 500 freshwater lochs in Lewis there might be a grain of truth as to this derivation of Lewis.

Stornoway (Gaelic: Steornabhagh) is said to be from the Norse for Steering Bay, which is acceptable from a Norse viewpoint. The name also appeared in 1511 as Stornochway, Steornway (1644) and Stornbay (1716). There is another Stornoway in Argyll which is in a bay very similar to its Lewis counterpart.

Harris (Gaelic: Na Hearadh) seems to indicate a place of high hills, or could indicate a district from the old Norse heradh, but this is in doubt. There is a Harris on the island of Rum and another on Islay. This name is best left to the scholars.

The following list is by no means exhaustive but gives some indication of how place-names indicate to some degree the topographical features of the area in which they occur. (N = Norse, G = Gaelic.)

Place–names	Derivation	Meaning
Aignish	N. eggnis	ridge-ness
Arnish	N. Ari-nis	Ari's headland
Back	N. bakki	ridge
Balallan	G. baile Ailein	Alan's town
Bayble	N. papa-boeli	land-locked but open to the sea
Bernera	N. Bjorn-vik	Bjorn's bay
Borve	N. borg	fort
Breascleit	N. breidr-klettr	broad crag or rock
Brenish	N. breidrnis	broad-ness
Brevig	N. breidr	broad bay
Calanais	N. Kalinis	Kali's headland
Coll	N. kula	rounded hill
Dell	N. dalr	dale
Garrabost	N. gard-bost	enclosed farm
Habost	N. har-bost	high farm
Kneep	N. gnipa	a peak
Keose	N. kjos	deep or hollow place
Langavat	N. langr-vatn	long loch
Laxdale	N. lax-dalr	salmon dale
Lionel	N. lin-dalr	flax dale
Obbe (Leverburgh)	N. hop	land-locked but open to the sea
Pabbay	N. Papa-ey	Priest's Isle
Scarasta	N. Skari-stadir	Skari's farm
Shader	N. stadir	farm
Steinish	N. steinnis	headland of the stones
Tolsta	N. Toli-stadir	Toli's farm
Tong	N. tunga	tongue of land
Uig	N. vik	bay or creek

FURTHER READING

Angus, S. *The Outer Hebrides: The Shaping of the Islands* (White Horse Press, 1997)

Armit, I. *The Archaeology of Skye and the Western Isles* (Edinburgh University Press,1996)

Ashmore, P. *Callanish: The Standing Stones* (Historic Scotland, 1996)

Buchanan, J. *The Lewis Land Struggle* (Acair, 1996)

Cunningham, P. *Birds of the Outer Hebrides* (Acair, 1990)

Hunter, J. *The Making of the Crofting Community* (John Donald, 1976)

Macaulay, J. *Silent Tower: St Clement's, Rodel* (Pentland Press, 1993)

Macaulay, M. *Aspects of the Religious History of Lewis*

Parker, J. *Walks in the Western Isles* (HMSO, 1996)

Thompson, F. *Lewis and Harris* (David & Charles, 1973)

Thompson, F. *Crofting Years* (Luath Press, 1997)

INDEX

Page numbers in *italic* indicate illustrations

One of the many stunning sunsets looking across to the now-deserted island of Taransay, Harris, from the Harris mainland